How to Live
Like a Gentleman

Sam Martin is the best-selling author of *How to Mow the Lawn* and *How to Keep House*. Sam has worked as a senior editor at *This Old House* magazine and is a contributing editor at *Budget Living* magazine. He lives in Texas with his wife Denise, and sons Ford and Wren.

How to Live
Like a Gentleman

LESSONS IN LIFE,
MANNERS, AND STYLE

Sam Martin

THE LYONS PRESS

An imprint of The Globe Pequot Press

Guilford, Connecticut

Copyright © 2007 by Elwin Street Limited
First Lyons Press edition, 2008

Conceived and produced by
Elwin Street Limited
144 Liverpool Road
London N1 1LA

The Lyons Press is an imprint of The Globe Pequot Press.

10 9 8 7

Designed by Jon Wainwright, Alchemedia Design
Illustrated by Micca/Dutch Uncle
Picture credits: The Advertising Archives pp48, 96; The Bridgeman Art Library p30; Mary
Evans Picture Library pp12, 76; Mary Evans Picture Library/Alamy p110
While every effort has been made to acknowledge copyright holders, Elwin Street Limited
would like to apologize for any omissions.

Printed in Singapore

ISBN 978-1-59921-351-4

Library of Congress Cataloging-in-Publication data is available on file.

CONTENTS

FOREWORD
BY RICK FINK, ENGLISH BUTLER

When I opened my school for butlers at the turn of the millennium, it was with the intention of retaining the old standards with which I was brought up. In my mind, knowledge of good manners and proper behavior was disappearing fast, and I wanted to try in my own small way to bring some of it back. I thought if I could just train a few people to take on these skills, they would be able to pass them on in turn, and then in time some of the old standards might return, like a classic style that after many years sees the light of day again.

You may wonder why a butler should need to know the skills of being a gentleman, when his job is only to serve one. Well there's a bit more to it than that: It is often the butler and his family who look after the children in a stately home. The gentleman's offspring often spend their early years in the butler's cottage or apartment, often eating and watching television with the butler and his family, and following all the different tasks that the butler undertakes. These children will one day become the owners of these estates, and it's not just private schools who teach them their manners and good behavior. The butler, his wife, and his own children have a hand in nurturing the next Lord of the Manor and helping him on his way to becoming a perfect gentleman.

Having been a gentleman's gentleman for fifty-three years, I can honestly say it has been a privilege to have been employed by some of the best in the land, and it has taught me the skills which I am now passing on to others. Many of the gentlemanly attributes mentioned in this book are qualities that I have especially noted throughout my years as a butler. I remember, for example, the wit and kindness of one gentleman for whom I worked in the 1950s. I once asked him, "Why is it, sir, that you always say no when I first ask you for something, and then a little later change your mind and say yes?" He said, "Well, if I said yes first off and then said no later, you would be most unhappy and think me cruel. But if I say no first and then change my mind to yes, you will think what a nice man I am!" This was true gentlemanly behavior: he allowed himself time to think, and made sure that, whatever his decision, he always came across as a gentleman.

In the twenty-first century, the benefits of multicultural societies and less rigid class structures have brought with them confusion about the correct way to behave. It has fallen upon a few of us who remember the old traditions to ensure that they are not entirely lost. I feel sure that this book is another way of showing that there are still people who care about, and want to try and bring back, some of these proper standards.

TO BE A GENTLEMAN—A REAL AND TRUE GENTLEMAN—A MAN SHOULD BE:

1. Of outstanding character.
2. Never late.
3. Always discreet.
4. Never arrogant.
5. Of impeccable manners.
6. Always well-spoken.
7. Immaculately dressed at all times.
8. Possessed of good social skills.
9. Possessed of genuine concern for others.
10. Forthright enough never to make excuses.

INTRODUCTION: MANNERS MATTER

A generation ago, a young man looking to live in refined confidence had to have been born with a silver spoon in his mouth. European nannies and etiquette schools would have shown him just what to do with that spoon, where to place it in the table setting, and how to use it without slurping. He would then have been shown the proper way to dress, talk, and act. Add to the equation some fine clothes, a svelte pad, and a sweet car—the perks of the monied class—and these young lads were well on their privileged way to becoming gentlemen.

Today, some of that scenario still holds true—a few of those lucky enough to be born into money still pay attention to the rigors of good etiquette. But these days, money is no guarantee of manners. Witness the lotto winner or the online trader who struck gold overnight, but wouldn't know when to give a toast and when to butter it. For some men, the idea of holding a door open for a lady is as mysterious as the looks they get while having a cell phone conversation at the opera. It's manners—those social refinements and thoughtful acts of kindness—that make any man a gentleman, regardless of the size of his wallet.

Even so, some men may wonder why manners matter at all. Can't we keep to ourselves, do what we do, and let everyone else be damned? Well, no, we can't, at least not in public. If no one took any notice of etiquette—that conscious attention to how we look, sound, and act around others—then the social fabric of crowded cities, overstuffed airplanes, romantic encounters, and stressed-out offices would disintegrate into rude chaos. We'd all be at each others' throats. No one would do business with us. We'd be poor, lonely, and sad. Good manners and a knowledge of etiquette ensure this doesn't happen.

A CHANGING LANDSCAPE FOR MEN

A knowledge of manners and etiquette also paves the path to manhood. Being a man requires a certain amount of experience and knowledge. Our greatest role models have always been men who were admired by their peers, who could forge an agreement in the most acrimonious atmosphere, and who knew how to treat a lady. Self-confidence, good manners, and kindness were their hallmarks. They were gentlemen.

Granted, today the social landscape is not what it used to be. Gender roles have changed and continue to change dramatically. Politics and the workplace are no longer exclusively male domains. Women now outnumber men attending and graduating from places of higher education. Even dating and romance have changed. Women no longer depend on men for financial support and worldly guidance. The women who are competing with men—and winning—at school and in the workplace are also looking for dates on the weekend. The message couldn't be clearer: if you want to be a successful gentleman in this new landscape, you have to know how to act, how to dress, how to talk, and how to date. You need to learn the new etiquette.

SELF-CONFIDENCE

It's one thing to say we need to change how we act, but it's another thing to do it. Etiquette is more than knowledge, it's a product of well-rooted self-confidence. After all, how we feel about ourselves is often how we present ourselves to others. If you honestly believe you can excel at a job or in a football game then that confidence will come through when you talk to your boss or walk into the huddle. People notice and reward good etiquette.

If you lack self-confidence, the good news is it can be built up with a little practice. You might have the urge to change your self-image by simply thinking differently but that's the hard way up. If you think of yourself as a nervous person, then telling yourself not to be nervous usually results in nervousness. Instead, the going theory is that changing behavior (i.e. refining your manners) is the better way to get a handle on things. When you feel like the butterflies are going to paralyze you, breathe deeply and speak slowly. If you aren't having any luck with the ladies or no one will give you a job, look at the sections in this book on personal hygiene and restaurant etiquette, and focus on looking professional and sharpening your wine knowledge instead of on what went wrong on the last interview or date.

PUTTING THE GENTLE BACK INTO THE MAN

Make no mistake, believing in yourself is one step to becoming a gentleman but it's not the only one. There are skills to hone, and they aren't the skills your father may have known. The new landscape calls for a new etiquette and a new type of gentleman. Call it old-fashioned chivalry combined with a modern respect for women.

When men talk to other men of confidence and respect, there is a tendency to resort to primordial male qualities like toughness and insensitivity. But becoming a gentleman does not mean regressing to our Neanderthal past. Current trends celebrate retro male values, but the real meaning of the saying "it's okay to be a man" is that men are capable of many dimensions. Translation: be proud of who you are. A gentleman with manners does not have to have feminine qualities. In fact, just the opposite. Putting the gentle back into man means nurturing the classic male qualities of kindness and thoughtfulness, patience, and trustworthiness.

It is in the spirit of these classic qualities that this book has been written. In these pages you'll find indispensable advice on how to cultivate your manners and etiquette to become successful beyond any financial gains. Learn everything from how to speak in front of large

Top Ten Qualities to Nurture

1   Competence—Knowledge breeds power.

2   Patience—An even keel will bring long life.

3   Resolve—Always follow through and you'll earn other people's respect.

4   Respect—Treat others with the same respect you hold for yourself.

5   Self-assurance—Being sure of what you do allows others to be sure of who you are.

6   Spirit—Laughter is the fountain of youth.

7   Diplomacy— Making friends is harder but more rewarding than making enemies.

8   Courage—Never be afraid of failure.

9   Trustworthiness—Do what you say and say what you do.

10   Constitution—Persistence pays.

groups to how to host a romantic dinner for two. There's information on how to woo women respectfully (do it with gusto), how to have a business lunch without making a mess of yourself (don't order lobster), and how to throw a successful bachelor party (do it with care). So while a fine suit will win you style points, don't hang your fedora on your looks and your bank account alone. Tip the dealer after the final hand, speak softly in foreign countries, never sip coffee from a spoon, and always offer your seat to a lady. She could, after all, turn out to be your next boss.

CHAPTER
1

STEPPING
OUT

IN THIS CHAPTER YOU'LL LEARN

❧ How to make a great first impression ❧ The tricks of meeting and greeting
❧ How to impress with small talk ❧ How to really impress when speaking
in public ❧ The proper way to behave on the phone and online

THE FIRST IMPRESSION

Looking sharp is a big part of living like a gentleman but it's not rule number one. The first thing you need to know is how to act like a man. Without a good handshake, solid posture, and eloquent conversation skills, you can wear the sharpest suit money can buy but you'll be wearing it alone. Knowing how to handle your social responsibilities with aplomb, on the other hand, will get you firmly on the path to gentlemanly living.

Every dating service, career coach, and image consultant on the planet agrees: how you first establish yourself with others is the key to any relationship. In fact, presenting a good first impression is the most important step on the path to good manners. Fairly or unfairly, in this post-feminist landscape, people are going to judge you to be a gentleman or not within the first minute or two of meeting you. Some say people can make conclusive judgements about a person within seconds. That's why bad first impressions will doom a job interview or blind date before it even gets started. However long it takes for someone to check you out for the first time, just don't give them any easy targets. For starters, know how to introduce yourself: confidence, style, and genuine friendliness will ensure that anybody's first impression of you is a good one.

THE HANDSHAKE

Changing landscape or not, the hallmark of any gentleman is his firm handshake. In fact, a good firm grip may be the most important impression you leave with someone—at least in the Western world. In places like Japan, for example, bowing replaces handshakes. In India and many Muslim countries, always shake with the right hand—left hands are reserved for toilet paper duties! These days, in countries where handshakes are common, it's appropriate to shake both men's and women's hands upon first encounters, especially business encounters.

BE A GENTLEMAN: HOW TO GIVE A GOOD GRIP

- ☑ Be close enough to the person whose hand you want to shake that you can stand up straight and comfortably extend your hand without having to lean over.

- ☑ Extend your entire hand to the person and look them in the eye.

- ☑ While continuing to look them in the eye, squeeze their hand, palm to palm with a firm grasp.

- ☑ If you feel comfortable doing it, shake the hand up and down at least once but not more than three times and then let go. It's perfectly acceptable to give a firm grip for a couple of seconds and let go without any pumping action.

- ☑ While you're shaking and making eye contact, be sure to smile and give a good positive greeting.

MIND YOUR MANNERS: WHAT TO AVOID WHEN SHAKING HANDS

[X] Don't squeeze someone's hand so hard that you crush it. Rather than coming off as strong and determined, it leaves the impression of a lack of confidence.

[X] Another no-no is grabbing someone's hand and pulling it toward you. It's controlling and overbearing and might alienate your new acquaintance.

[X] Enveloping a handshake by putting your free hand on top of the other person's hand during a handshake is good if you're seeing an old friend but not okay when meeting someone for the first time. It's too personal and some people will be put off by it.

[X] There are a few styles of shake that will doom you from the word go. One is the limp shake, by which you just hold out your hand but don't squeeze. If you're on the giving end, this feels similar to firmly grabbing a flabby, lifeless tenderloin steak. It's unpleasant, to say the least.

[X] Don't hold out your hand lazily. Chances are you'll get your fingers crushed. Not only does this hurt, it's wimpy.

[X] The most infamous bad shake is the dead fish or the clammy hand. This is a combination of the limp shake and the sweaty palm. If your hand is wet—either from nervousness or from holding a cold drink—dry it before greeting.

THE GREETING

How you should say hello will often depend on the circumstances. Going on a job interview or business trip is going to be different than greeting someone who has come over for dinner at your house. For the former you might want to say something like: "Hello, my name is Sam Martin. I'm with ABC company." In more casual environments, no one's going to be interested in your job, at least not right away. For any occasion, nothing beats a genuine smile and solid eye contact. If you're stressed or angry and you let that show on your face, others will pick up on it and feel as though they're not welcome. For that matter, letting your eyes wander around the room or over a person's shoulder might give the impression that you're waiting for someone more interesting. A gentleman will want his new acquaintances to know he is pleased to meet them and genuinely happy to have them around.

A simple greeting is best. Stand up when you meet someone, give them a good smile, a firm handshake, and say who you are. If you walk into a room, approach the others and introduce yourself immediately.

WHAT TO SAY WHEN

After you say "hello" or "hi" and give your first and last name, here are a few scenarios and suggestions of what you can say.

- In almost any situation: "*Pleasure to meet you.*"

- At a job interview: "*Thanks for your time.*"
  or "*I've been looking forward to our meeting.*"

- New friends coming over for dinner: "*Glad you could make it.*"

- On a blind date: "*Thanks for meeting me.*"
  or "*You look great.*"

THE HELLO KISS

Not everyone gets a hello kiss and those that do usually aren't expecting a smacker on the lips. A cheek to cheek kiss in the air or a small peck on the jaw is the appropriate approach to this most European of greetings that's usually reserved for more familiar friends. That said, if you're in Europe—Paris especially—don't wince or pull away when greeted by a total stranger with a cheek kiss. When in Rome do as the Romans do. The same can be said closer to home. If a lady friend or acquaintance makes the move for a hello kiss, give her your best one. This isn't a sensual event. It's a gentlemanly skill that will give you an added air of confidence and sophistication.

WALKING AND POSTURE

The language of the body is as important as what you say. Many a snap judgement has been made after seeing a man slouch in his chair at dinner or shuffle his feet through the office door. A gentleman should always keep his back straight, his shoulders back, and his chin up (those engaging in the occasional sparring match should do just the opposite). Walking too can reveal a sense of self-worth and confidence. If you want to make an impression when entering a room, keep your eyes up and move with purpose towards your destination. If you're sitting at dinner or at a business meeting, don't lean back in your chair—it gives the impression that you're bored. So does jiggling a knee, tapping a foot, or staring around the room instead of at the person talking. If you're standing, rocking back and forth on your feet can make you seem anxious to get away. Crossing your arms has the subtle effect of making you standoffish while open arms, or hands on a table when seated, suggests you're open for business.

MEETING PEOPLE

Men who walk into a room with purpose and greet others with bright eyes and a firm handshake won't have a problem meeting people. Unless they stop there. Those with energetic greetings need to have polished conversation skills to talk the talk.

SMALL TALK

Small talk is often criticized for being trite and insincere but one has to start somewhere. Launching immediately into an exposition of the Peloponnesian War will more likely dim others' interest than pique it. Wait for cocktails for that one. At first, engage in a little get-to-know-you exchange. Ask questions like "how do you know the host?" "do you have plans for the holidays?" "how was your vacation?" and "did

---

MIND YOUR MANNERS: A GENTLEMAN WOULD NEVER SAY

- ☒ "How's your ex?"
- ☒ "Do you have plans for Christmas?" (Not everyone celebrates Christmas.)
- ☒ "Do you dye your hair?"
- ☒ "When's your due date?" (What if they're not pregnant?)
- ☒ "I found a hair in my soup."
- ☒ "I hate coming to these things, don't you?"

you grow up around here?" Usually, the answers you get and give will lead to more. Listen carefully so you can develop these entrées into more in-depth conversation. If nothing strikes you, the best way to ensure an ongoing, vibrant conversation is to keep asking questions. Just avoid dead-end queries that can be answered in "yes" or "no." People love talking about themselves. A gentleman should never spend too much time talking about himself.

INTRODUCING PEOPLE TO OTHERS

Often gentlemen will travel in numbers. If you're in the know and the rest of your posse is in the dark, it's up to you to illuminate them. At parties you'll want to introduce friends to the host and other important people. At business gatherings, seek out the decision makers. When introducing people, first say the name of the person you're meeting followed by your introduction. The exchange might go something like this: "Ed, I'd like you to meet a friend/business associate/(fill in the blank) of mine, John Smith." If you know the two share a common interest or goal it's completely appropriate and encouraged to make that connection for them. "John just got back from a cycling trip in the Pyrénées," you might say. "Ed does a lot of cycling himself." You know you've done a good job if you find yourself excluded from the conversation, leaving you free to withdraw politely and meet new people of your own.

If the two people you've introduced don't have much in common or are having trouble connecting, it's up to you to gracefully end the conversation. Take your leave by saying something like "Nice talking you, Ed. We'll see you around." Always walk away with the person you brought into the conversation in the first place, so they don't feel like you've ditched them.

DICTION AND ELOQUENCE

Small talk and social conversation skills are one thing, but a gentleman socializing in this new landscape of easily accessible information and highly educated men and women should be as comfortable in serious discussion as in chitchat. Conversing with the most accomplished speakers requires a facility with language and a good vocabulary that does not rely on "um," "like," or "whatever." Respect in the boardroom or in front of a packed house is not dependent on broad shoulders and good looks, but on a familiarity with the etiquette of talking to others, the cornerstones of which are preparation and knowledge.

SPEAKING CLEARLY

No matter how eloquent, a gentleman will never impress unless he can speak clearly and loudly enough for others to hear. You don't need a background in theater to achieve this but the notion of projecting the voice like an actor can be helpful. Don't mumble. Keep your hand away from your mouth when you speak. If you're in front of a large audience, speak to the person in the back row to ensure your voice is loud enough.

VOCABULARY

Choose your words carefully when speaking, and use a sophisticated vocabulary to reveal the finer points of your argument. Anyone who can articulate an idea with appropriate terminology commands respect by showing a deeper understanding of the subject and a facility with language. It allows them to communicate more effectively. Plus, if you're listening to others talk you don't want to get caught flat-footed with a word you don't know. For those starting out with a limited supply of words, get out a thesaurus and a dictionary and start looking up words you use often. These are likely to be words associated with your profession, hobbies, and interests. A little free writing will help. Just write down a word and try to think of several others that put a finer point on its meaning—looking them up in the thesaurus is appropriate. Preparing yourself like this before a big speech or even before a social outing can afford less than vociferous neophytes with meretricious elocution skills in no time.

PUBLIC SPEAKING

Talking in front of others is a learned skill that improves over time. Gentlemen who do this well exhibit the same manners they might in more intimate settings: wit, confidence, and awareness of others. Brevity is also an admirable goal: if you can use one word instead of three and still make yourself understood, use the one.

If you've been asked to speak to a large crowd, it's because you have something to offer and an agreeable manner with which to present your ideas—confident thoughts you can remember to calm any first-time speaking nerves. Nonetheless it's always daunting to stand up and make yourself heard. Luckily there are studied public speaking methods you can tuck into your portfolio before taking the podium.

BE A GENTLEMAN: KNOW YOUR MATERIAL INSIDE AND OUT

- ☑ Know what your audience wants and tailor your talk to them.

- ☑ Practice your speech in front of a mirror before you hit the stage.

- ☑ Don't be glued to your notes. Instead establish a rapport with your crowd by making frequent eye contact, using hand gestures, and relating personal examples of what you're discussing.

- ☑ Slow down and speak clearly, pausing to bring weight to the key points.

- ☑ Be funny, especially if your subject can get overly technical or philosophical.

- ☑ Consider using visual aids or handouts but avoid digital presentations unless they do more than just reveal bullet points of things you're already saying.

- ☑ Finally, know when to stop talking. This is really dependent on crafting an efficient speech with good vocabulary so that your point is presented as succinctly as possible.

LESSONS IN LISTENING

For the modern gentleman it's not enough to be good with words. You must also know how to listen. A good listener shows that they are both engaged in the topic of conversation and interested in the speaker's thoughts and opinions on it—both keys to good manners. Listening means not only hearing the words but understanding the concepts behind them.

A good listener hears with purpose. He interprets what he's heard by paraphrasing a point or idea back to the speaker. He asks questions to dig deeper into the conversation. He avoids judging a person or their ideas and instead he uses what he knows and what he has

MIND YOUR MANNERS: POLITE LISTENING

- [X] Never finish the speaker's sentences for them.
- [X] Don't talk and talk and talk so they can't get a word in edgeways. Remember this is dialogue, not monologue.
- [X] Don't look around the room instead of looking at the speaker in the eye.
- [X] Don't interrupt to take a cell phone call, say hi to passersby, or pet a small animal.
- [X] Don't analyze last night's dream sequences.
- [X] Never imagine the speaker naked, no matter how attractive.
- [X] Try not to daydream.

experienced to understand the speaker's point of view. He might challenge or debate with this opinion but he won't dismiss it out of hand, and he'll never let debate descend into argument.

Of course, there will be occasions when even the most well-mannered gentleman is less enamoured of the topic of conversation than his interlocutor—in other words, he gets bored. While it's bad manners to let someone know you find their conversation dull, by directly telling them, or indirectly by looking bored and fidgeting, it's perfectly acceptable for a gentleman to steer the topic of conversation towards areas he finds more interesting. And if all else fails, a gentleman can politely take his leave by asking for directions to the bathroom.

LISTENING FOR PUBLIC SPEAKING

Often people make the mistake that they don't have to listen to their audiences during a crowded presentation. Not true. Just as at an intimate social event, listening in public speaking is the key to gauging feedback. One shouldn't give in to a drunk heckler at the back of the room, but grumblings or questions from the crowd should not be ignored. A well-mannered gentleman will engage his critics in public with the same self-confidence he brings to more friendly environments.

Above all, be alert to the reaction you get from your audience and try and tailor your speech and manner to fit. Look out for people yawning, fidgeting, or just looking bored, and try to recapture their interest by directing a few points directly to them. If you sense that one topic isn't going down well, change tack and skip to the next point in your speech. And if everybody in the room is half asleep, do yourself and them a favor and just skip to the end.

PHONE AND ONLINE ETIQUETTE

CELL PHONES

Cell phones are so ubiquitous now that most people have gotten used to others chatting while in public. This doesn't mean it's always done in good taste.

CALL WAITING

If you have call waiting, it doesn't mean you always have to use it. It's great not to miss a call, but if you're in the middle of an important discussion why interrupt it? Ideally your voice mail will field the beep so you can continue the conversation at hand. If you must put someone on hold, do so politely but quickly and get back to the conversation as soon as you can. The way to do this is to say "I have another call, do you mind if I put you on hold for a second?" Then field the other call and simply say, "Hi, I'm in the middle of a conversation, can I call you back?" Ending the initial call for one coming through on call waiting is not appropriate, unless you've warned your caller first that you're expecting an important call and may have to run.

BEEPERS

The same rules that apply to cell phone rings apply to beepers. Turn them off or switch them to vibrate in restaurants, performances, meetings, or classes. If you're a doctor, responding to a beeper call is usually understandable. If you're not a doctor, only the most pressing circumstances should pry you out of a movie or a romantic dinner for two.

BE A GENTLEMAN: USING YOUR CELL PHONE

☑ Be aware of those around you and try not to invade their audio space, even when you're outside. Nothing ruins a sunset more than the sound of a ringing telephone.

☑ Be conscious of the people you're hanging out with as well, especially if you're on a date. Talking on the phone to someone about the day's sports scores means you're ignoring the person you're with, and who wants to be ignored?

☑ Turn your phone off before going into restaurants, performances, or waiting rooms. If you have to be available during these times, make sure you have a phone with a vibrating signal and always get up and walk outside before you take the call.

☑ Don't talk on the phone while driving. Some studies have equated driving while talking on the phone to driving while drunk. That's how absent a driving cell phone talker can be behind the wheel. Not only is it bad etiquette, it's dangerous.

NETIQUETTE

With the explosion of blogs, texting, online chats, and e-mail, the need for a new kind of etiquette on the net—netiquette—is yet another symptom of the changing landscape for gentlemen. Just because you can't see or directly talk to the person you're communicating with doesn't mean you shouldn't be cordial and charming. A sharp wit is fine but outright insults don't make you tough or smart—they make you uninteresting. No one's going to read a blog or chat if the content consists entirely of snide remarks.

Perhaps the most used form of electronic communication is e-mail. It's not like talking on the phone but it's far from sending an old-fashioned letter. The mistake many people make is being too casual in e-mails to people they don't know very well. You don't have to compose a formal letter each time you ping someone but using the same shorthand you use when texting a buddy over the phone isn't always appropriate either. A general rule of thumb is always start and end the first e-mail of the day to someone with a formal greeting and sign off. "Hi, Steve" to start and "All the best, Sam" to end is fine. Then if the two of you get into some back and forth it's okay to drop the formal greeting.

The challenge with cell phones and portable e-mail is having the willpower to not answer every message or call the moment it comes in. Work and communication can be addictive, but ignoring people you're with while you play with your phone is not an attractive habit. Reserve some time when you're on your own for interacting with electronics, and keep face-to-face relationships healthy. If you absolutely must respond to an e-mail or text message, apologize to your companions and try to do it discreetly and quickly.

BE A GENTLEMAN: SAVVY E-MAILING

✓ Avoid sending messages in all lowercase letters—they make you look like you have no self-esteem. Avoid messages all in capitals, which make you appear angry.

✓ Always respond to e-mails you get, even if it's just to say "I got it, thanks."

✓ Check spelling, grammar, and punctuation carefully.

✓ Don't send attachments that are so big it will take a day to download them.

✓ Limit or stop sending chain letters or jokes. Who has time to read these things?

Chapter 2

HYGIENE, GROOMING, AND DRESS

IN THIS CHAPTER YOU'LL LEARN

✦ The importance of personal hygiene ✦ Tips for shaving ✦ The mysteries of ironing ✦ How to develop your own style ✦ What to include in the perfect wardrobe and when to wear it ✦ How to choose and wear a suit and tie ✦ Essential accessories for the stylish gentleman

PERSONAL HYGIENE

What are the first things you think of when you hear the word "gentleman"? Chances are a fine suit is in there somewhere, maybe even a top hat and tails, if you're the old-fashioned type. Men's fashion has come on a long way since those were in style but a modern gentleman still has to know how to look the part. Here are a few tips to make sure your image matches up to your gentlemanly manners.

Wandering nose hairs or a bush sprouting from each ear do not add to a good first impression. Neither does an unkempt coif. Gentlemen aren't required to spend huge sums stocking up on the latest skincare products (though one or two might be a good addition), but they are required to pay attention to the cut of their hair—whether short or long, especially long—shower every day, and spend some time in front of the bathroom mirror. This is especially true, though somewhat surprising, for gentlemen graduating into their thirties. Whatever his age, a gentleman's care for his appearance starts long before he dresses, with a shower, shave, and a little styling. You might even consider treating yourself to some professional attention once a year: facial, exfoliation, pumice scrub, clay mask, manicure, and pedicure are all more fun than they sound.

Be a Gentleman: Hygiene Checklist

Daily

- [x] Wash underarms, feet, and nether regions.
- [x] Examine face and neck for burgeoning pimples.
- [x] Rub lotion on cracked, dry hands.
- [x] Shave.

As needed

- [x] Examine nose hair length and trim as needed with small scissors.
- [x] Look for ear hairs and pluck them with tweezers. Shaving or scissoring only encourages shrub-like growth.
- [x] Check and tweeze eyebrows threatening uni-brow domination.
- [x] Attend to neck hair or back hair peeking above the collar line by shaving or trimming.
- [x] Trim fingernails.

SHAVING

A good shave shows. Granted, a two- or three-day stubble can make a man look and feel cool, as if he's been shut away painting his masterpiece or out in the Yukon forests tracking grizzlies. But first impressions are best made with a clean face, especially when courting (women or employers). For gentlemen cultivating an old-fashioned style, a straight razor is the way to go. But these days there are so many shaving products to choose from that one doesn't need to bother with a leather strop and a mug of shaving cream. In any case, the technique is going to be the same.

WHAT TO DO IF YOU CUT YOURSELF

Cutting yourself while shaving is unfortunate but it comes with the territory. Luckily the modern gentleman has access to various techniques to stop the bleeding, which unchecked can last for 15 minutes after a hot shower. The best is a "styptic pencil," which contains a medicine that stops blood flow by contracting blood vessels. You can buy them from drugstores. Or you can put a drop of medical alcohol or a dab of petroleum jelly on a cotton swab and use it to apply pressure on the cut.

MIND YOUR MANNERS: CONCEAL SHAVING CUTS

- [X] Never put tiny bits of toilet paper on the cuts and go out in public.
- [X] Don't let the blood clot into a large prominent scab before a date.
- [X] Don't just do nothing and let the blood flow as you're leaving the house.

HOW TO SHAVE

You will need

- ☑ Small towel
- ☑ Hot water
- ☑ Razor
- ☑ Shaving cream/soap
- ☑ Aftershave lotion

1 Wash your face with hot water and facial soap.

2 Wet a small towel with hot water (as hot as you can stand it) and use this as a hot pack on your face for about two minutes. The water and the heat help soften tough facial hair.

3 After the hot pack has been removed, rub the shaving cream or soap of your choice on your face. A shaving brush can be a sophisticated alternative to using your hands, and helps facial hair stand up a bit better.

4 Shave the sideburns first, to allow the soap to soak into your chin and upper lip (the tougher areas of a beard). Do not shave upward or against the growth of the hair. When the sideburns are done, shave the cheeks, then the sides of the neck, the center of the neck, the upper lip, the lower lip, and finally the chin. Rinse the razor after each pass.

5 Rinse your face with hot water. One last splash of cold water helps close pores.

6 Apply an alcohol-based aftershave astringent or lotion to keep your face from getting irritated.

IRONING

It's a fact that wearing wrinkled shirts and trousers looks bad. Nowadays, with a dry cleaner on every block and women in every office wearing perfectly pressed power suits, a modern gentleman needs to take these details seriously. There are three solutions. One is to have your personal man-servant do the ironing. Another is to take all your shirts and pants to the cleaners once a week, perfectly acceptable, if only slightly less expensive than hiring a man-servant. The best solution is to iron your clothes yourself.

How to Iron a Shirt
and a Pair of Trousers

You will need

✓	Iron filled with distilled water (for steam)
✓	Ironing board

Shirt

1	Set the iron temperature to the correct setting (irons usually have settings based on the type of material you're pressing). Linen shirts can get singed and will turn brown in spots if the iron is too hot. Then you have a bigger problem than wrinkles.
2	To iron a shirt so that you don't wrinkle it as you go, spread the shirt flat on the ironing board and press the back of the collar first.

continued on next page

3	Flip it over and press the front of the collar. Iron from the ends toward the center as collars tend to crease.
4	Next, open up the cuffs and iron them, insides first and then the outsides.
5	Iron the sleeves next. Lay them flat on the board and smooth them out so you don't press any creases in the material. Iron in slow deliberate movements, smoothing and straightening as you go. Don't leave the iron in one place too long as it can burn the material.
6	To iron the shoulders, fit the arm holes on the end of the board.
7	Iron the body of the shirt last. Lay the shirt so that the collar points toward the narrow end of the board and one front side of the shirt lays flat on the board. Iron from the shoulder to the shirt tails.
8	Rotate the shirt. Iron the back next and the other front side last.

Trousers

1	Set the iron to the correct temperature for the material of the pants.
2	Determine whether you want pants with a crease or without.
3	Pants with a crease will likely already have one in them. Lay the pants flat on the ironing board and iron it out.
4	Iron the crease back in by lining up the seams and laying the pants flat on the ironing board with one leg on top of the other.
5	When you've done one leg, fold it back and iron the other.
6	Fold the other leg back down and iron it.
7	Flip the pants over and repeat.
8	After that, hang the pants up until it's time to put them on.

IMAGE: THE IMPORTANCE OF DEVELOPING YOUR OWN STYLE

Gentlemen throughout history have cultivated an image for themselves that made them instantly recognizable and able to stand out in a crowd. There's no reason to believe the modern gentleman can't do the same. Your particular style, whatever it may be, is like a personal silent announcement when you meet someone. It shows a gentleman's attention to detail and a savvy handle on the importance of leaving a lasting impression.

DRESSING FOR RESPECT

Some gentlemen have a sense of gravitas about them that draws people in and commands instant respect. Walking into a room with good posture, a bright smile, and a confident stride will go a long way toward cultivating this respect. Wearing the right clothes, however, will drive the point home. One doesn't have to wear a suit and tie to gain the admiration of others but one does have to look sharp and dressed for the occasion. A gentleman wouldn't want to wear flip-flops to a company party. Nor would he throw on a pair of shorts to go to the opera. These are the kind of choices which, while not altogether grounds for social dismissal, would not foster the respect of others. Ironed shirts and pants, on the other hand, would. As would up to date fashion. It's hard to look admirably upon a man wearing a Members Only jacket, even if it is supposed to be ironic.

MIND YOUR MANNERS: WHAT NOT TO WEAR

- ☒ Flip-flops to a business meeting.
- ☒ All black to a wedding.
- ☒ All white to a funeral.
- ☒ Clothes to a nude beach.
- ☒ No clothes to a regular beach.
- ☒ A hat to the movies.
- ☒ White pants after Labor Day.
- ☒ A T-shirt on a first date.
- ☒ Berets, beanies, or head stockings.
- ☒ Anything baggy.

There are also certain dress-codes for specific occasions of which a gentleman should be aware. Some, such as a black tie or armband for a funeral, are still common. Others less so. In the olden days, for example, wearing all black to a wedding was taken to mean one disapproved of the match. Nowadays few people know or take any notice of this, but a gentleman might want to bear it in mind when choosing his outfit for the day to avoid any potential awkwardness.

THE PERFECT WARDROBE

Men don't need to be clotheshorses to look good for any occasion but it's important to update your wardrobe for the seasons. No hard and fast rules apply except that you shouldn't wear white before Easter or after Labor Day. Nor should you forget to slip on a pair of socks for nights out on the town or for important business meetings, no matter what time of year it is. Items such as shorts, flip-flops, and T-shirts should be carefully matched with the event. Also, a good suit—of navy blue, black, or gray—is always a necessity. A gentleman needs to be able to conquer the world any time of the year. Round out any wardrobe with cuff links, tie clips, watches, handkerchiefs, sunglasses, and a variety of black and brown belts.

BE A GENTLEMAN: A WARDROBE FOR ALL SEASONS...

. . . for winter

- ☑ A pair of boots you can wear through snow, slush, and mud, and arrive at your destination still looking good. Boots are great for day to day but not best for night outings or work.

- ☑ Bright scarves to liven up all the black and gray winter wear during the day or night.

- ☑ Soft, smooth, and seasoned leather gloves—not mittens or thick mountaineering numbers, so you can actually use your fingers when they're bundled. Use in the day but not at night when you're going in and out of bars or clubs. They'll get lost.

- ☑ Long wool coat—choose a black, navy, or gray coat so you never have to worry about coordinating with pants, shirts, or sweaters. Good for any occasion.

continued on next page

. . . for spring

- [x] Lightweight suede jacket for those chilly evening outings.
- [x] Dark designer jeans for work or going out with the guys.
- [x] Fitted dress shirts in a variety of bright spring colors for bright nightlife or weekend weddings.
- [x] Canvas boat shoes for afternoons in the park.

. . . for summer

- [x] Seersucker suit with white cotton shirt—perfect for summer weddings, gin and tonics after tennis, or a summer picnic or night out with your sweetie.
- [x] Straw boater for weddings or afternoon picnics.
- [x] Cargo shorts cut just above the knee for low-key outings.
- [x] Linen pants in white or cream for more upscale outings.

. . . for fall

- [x] Zip-up cardigan-style sweater in wool or cashmere.
- [x] Shirts in toned down colors of navy blue, gray, brown, or beige.
- [x] Corduroy pants for casual dates or work.
- [x] Versatile coat for rainy or cold weather that can be dressy and casual for everyday wear.
- [x] Lace-up or slip-on Oxford shoes and ankle boots that can be worn to work and a Friday night play.

SUITS

One thing that has not changed for gentlemen of recent generations is the essential nature of a fine suit. These days, a gentleman might not need more than one—suiting up for the office long ago went the way of the nine-to-five working day. But one good suit and a fine pair of leather dress shoes to match is a must. It will make a gentleman feel like a million bucks and give him that extra boost of confidence when he's trying to impress someone with his fine manners.

Shopping for a suit can be surprisingly overwhelming, not least because they can set you back $500 and sometimes much more. If this is your one and only suit, strongly consider getting a dark gray or navy blue one. They might be conservative but they will always work, winter, spring, or summer. Black suits make you look like you work for the Mafia or the CIA, so you should probably steer clear. You can get creative with second suits. Pinstripes might work for one-suit wardrobes, especially for those who are vertically challenged. But by the same token, if you're over six foot five, steer clear.

The style of suit is another consideration. Again, if this is your one and only suit, steer clear of elements that are overly fashionable and might go out of style the following year. Extra thin, overly large, or pointy lapels fall into this category, as do overly fitted coats and jackets. Stick with conservative lapels and slightly trim fits. As for two- or three-button suits, go for whichever fits your body style. Tall men look good in three-button suits whereas shorter men or those with small trunks should wear the two-button. You should only ever fasten one button on your suit jacket: the top one on a two-button, or the middle one on a three-button jacket.

You may also notice the "vents"—those slits cut into the back of the coat. American-made suits normally have one center vent where European tailors go for two—one on each side. Either is fine depending on your preference, although larger-waisted men may prefer the extra room to maneuver provided by the second vent. You can always get vents closed up by a tailor if you really don't like them.

Lastly, consider suit pants. You'll have one-pleat, two-pleat, and flat front to choose from. If you go flat front, skip the cuff. Pleated pant wearers can consider a single fold at the cuff, but never more than an inch and a half deep.

Almost anybody can buy a suit "off the peg" that will fit them and look at least reasonably good. However, if you're determined to stand out in your formal attire and money is no object, you might consider paying a couple of grand for a "bespoke" suit, that is, one made by a tailor to fit your exact body measurements. If you don't fancy this price tag but still want to look sharp, get a good tailor to work on a shop-bought suit. He should be able to alter the jacket and trousers for a perfect fit. It's still expensive, but it's worth it, adding the final touches to a gentleman's most ambitious outfit.

TIES

Of course, no suit would be complete without a tie. And guys, go ahead and splash out on a new tie each year. Perhaps the only thing worse than an out-of-style square-toed pair of dress shoes is an out-of-style tie. When you're wearing a suit your tie is the most prominent item of clothing; it shows off your individual style, so you should choose it carefully. Bounce your ideas off of someone—anyone—before cinching up and hitting the town: that green and purple plaid might look good in the store, but in the cold light of day it'll be less flattering. Start with subtle colors and patterns and do not wear shirts and ties in matching colors (that is so last century).

In general, most guys should go with a straight tie, tied with a Windsor knot. The end of your tie should just reach your belt buckle when you're standing up. Bow ties are another option, but they either look great or awful; rarely is there an in between. The exceptions are black-tie or formal events like weddings, where everyone is required to put one on to go with a tuxedo or morning suit. Outside of these situations, you risk looking like an eccentric professor or variety performer. But if you can pull off a bow tie when it isn't required, there are few items of clothing more unusual and therefore more liberating than this neckwear. For a gentleman looking to make an impression in the modern work-hard play-hard world, a bow tie is a bold step. Just be sure you know exactly what you're doing before you take it on.

How to Tie a Bow Tie

If you wear the clip-on type, stop. It'll take some practice but anyone can tie the real thing. A self-tied bow tie is the kind of detail that not everyone will notice, but will nonetheless make you feel like you can conquer the world.

You will need

 A bow tie

 Lots of patience

1   Drape the tie around your neck with the left-hand end (L) about two inches longer than the right (R).

2   Cross the L end over the top of the R end.

3   Bring the L end up and under the loop, pulling the tie snug against your neck and allowing the L end to hang down.

4   Fold the R end into a loop at the end of the tie and hold it between your thumb and forefinger. This will be the base of the bow.

5   Fold the L end into a loop similar to the R end and while holding the R end in place with one hand, bring the folded L end over the front and around the back of the R end, pushing the L end behind the R end.

6   Pull the two ends outward, tugging them with your fingers and straightening the center knot until you have a perfect "bow."

ESSENTIAL STYLISH ITEMS
TO LAST A LIFETIME

Clothes come and go with seasons and increasing waistlines but a few items in a gentleman's wardrobe will withstand the changing winds of fashion. It's worth paying for quality with items like these, since more expensive models tend to last longer. Designer labels are all very well, but go for the classic look to keep you in fashion as the years go by. Bear in mind that leather watch straps, belts, and shoes should all be in matching colors—black or brown for preference. Owning one belt of each color is a sensible precaution, but you might want to buy a watch with a metal strap—they can be worn with anything.

♦ A fine watch is always the sign of a responsible and responsibly stylish gentleman.

♦ A supple leather wallet or finely-crafted money clip will become a man's best friend.

♦ Cigar or cigarette smokers, even casual ones, will adore an initialed lighter or silver tobacco case to keep in a suit's breast pocket.

♦ Wool fedoras, gray wool cowboy hats, straw boaters, silk bowlers, or any other fine headwear will transcend the seasons.

♦ Cuff links are fine details any time of the year.

♦ A tie clip or pin can put the finishing touches on any man's finery, young or old.

FASHION DOS AND DON'TS
FROM HEAD TO TOE

Certainly there are some hard-and-fast rules about fashion but the one rule a gentleman should always heed is to wear clothes that he feels good in. A Paul Smith three-button suit is one of the world's finest articles of clothing but if you feel like a pretender when you put one on, it's not for you, no matter how fashionable it may be.

Fashion Dos

- ✓ Make sure your shoes and belt are the same color.
- ✓ Match sock color with pant color.
- ✓ Wear a white T-shirt or tank top under dress shirts.
- ✓ Wear metal watch bands—they go with everything.

Fashion Don'ts

- ✗ Don't wear white after Labor Day.
- ✗ Don't mix plaids with stripes.
- ✗ Don't wear white athletic socks unless you're being athletic.
- ✗ Don't wear the same color tie and shirt. It's out of fashion.
- ✗ Don't wear clip-on ties. Yes, learn to tie a bow tie.

CHAPTER
3

EATING
AND
DRINKING

IN THIS CHAPTER YOU'LL LEARN

✦ The importance of table manners ✦ The way to behave in a restaurant
✦ How to taste wine ✦ How to behave when drinking and when drunk
✦ How to host a party ✦ How to mix a cocktail ✦ How to be a
perfect guest (and get invited back)

TABLE MANNERS

You cannot prize good table manners too highly. They fall into the "small details" category that, correctly employed, always leave others with the impression of refinement. If you practice them consistently, not many people will notice your good manners but that's the point. You want people to listen to what you have to say rather than focus on whether or not you're chewing with your mouth open.

ELBOWS AND TABLES

One of the oldest table manners in the book is keep your elbows off. Elbows on is crude: it crowds the person sitting next to you, and it makes you hunch over your plate as if you haven't eaten in days. Before or after dinner it's acceptable to have an elbow on the table, especially if you're making a point during a conversation. When the food is served though, keep them both off.

USING A NAPKIN

Dealing with your napkin is often the first indication of good table manners. Not dealing with it is the indication of an unrefined diner. Once everyone in your party is seated, discreetly remove your napkin from the table top, fold it in half, and lay it across your lap. Etiquette sticklers will tell you the fold needs to be facing toward you but unless you're dining with your mother who may check such a thing, don't worry about this particular detail. If you have to get up in the middle of dinner, fold your napkin again (never reveal a wadded one) and place it in the seat of your chair. On returning pick it up and place it again in your lap. Only after dinner should you place the napkin back on the table next to your plate, never on your plate. Should you drop the linen to the floor within easy reach, pick it up. If it has fallen so far that you'd have to make a fool of yourself to retrieve it, just ask for another one.

EATING AND TALKING

Dinner with good conversation is a must for any gentleman or anyone who wants to get invited to the next party. That said, you don't want to spray your neighbor with a mouthful of steak au poivre. Take small bites that you can chew and swallow quickly so you can keep the conversation going. Never talk with food in your mouth.

WAIT TO EAT

Unless you've just come out of the jungle after three months eating leather belts and grubs, you should never tuck into dinner until everyone is seated and begins eating. Even if your steak goes from piping hot to frigid, don't do it. If there's water at the table, feel free to sip. When dinner arrives, a gentleman should wait until his host or date picks up their fork before picking up his, and wait until they begin to eat before even tasting the food in front of him. The exception to this rule is if the host or hostess asks you to start eating. In this case, go ahead.

BEING ON TIME

Timeliness is gentlemanliness. One should always be prompt especially to dinners and business meetings. Meeting a date on time is a way to show respect. Getting to a meeting five minutes before it starts is a way to show you're organized and engaged. Perhaps the only time it's okay not to be on time is when you've been invited to a late-night party. Even then you don't want to be the last person to show up—no one will notice you've arrived.

OUT ON THE TOWN

Now that you know basic table manners, it's time to explore a few of the better restaurants in town and practice your prowess with a napkin.

HOW TO ORDER IN A RESTAURANT

When it is time to choose your food, consider who you're with. On a romantic date, it's acceptable to discuss the menu with your partner and then order for the both of you. It's not okay to order for someone without discussing food first, especially if you're with someone you don't know well. Lamb shanks won't win you kudos if she's a

---

MIND YOUR MANNERS: RESTAURANT BEHAVIOR

- [X] Don't raise your hand high in the air so that the server—and everyone else in the restaurant—can see it. Embarrassing your waiter will not speed things up.
- [X] Never snap your fingers or whistle at a server.
- [X] Likewise, never tap a waiter on the shoulder.
- [X] Try not to ask the server for something new every time he or she comes to the table to check on you. Eventually, they'll stop coming. Instead, think of everything you might need and ask for it all at once.
- [X] Don't get loud in a quiet setting.
- [X] Don't leave a bad tip.

Be a Gentleman: Dealing with Your Server

☑ Eye contact with a waiter or waitress is the most subtle and most suave way to get their attention. This can be punctuated by holding one finger up just in front of you.

☑ Ask questions instead of making demands.

☑ You know where you're going to eat long before you sit down at the table. Know what kind of food you're in the mood for—fish or steak?—so that you don't hold everyone else's dinner up. It'll also make your server's job easier.

☑ If you can't decide, let your server tell you what they recommend and then trust them on it.

☑ If your server is having a bad night and seems surly, keep smiling and stay calm even when they're not. Usually they'll relax with you. If things get really bad, say something to the manager only after you've finished eating and the bill is paid.

☑ Tip well. You'll earn a reputation for your generosity and the next time you go to that restaurant you and your guest will get treated well.

vegetarian. If you're on a business dinner, let the host take charge. If you're the host, go ahead and order a few appetizers—be sure to vary them between vegetarian and non-vegetarian. If you're dining formally, avoid food that's difficult to eat such as lobster or half a chicken. If you choose menu items that are difficult to pronounce, it's acceptable just to ask the server about it and point. No need to embarrass yourself by butchering a foreign language.

SENDING FOOD BACK

The rule with sending food back is don't do it unless you absolutely must. If you get completely the wrong meal, for example, let your server know discreetly right away so you can get the right meal before everyone else has finished. Small mistakes like the wrong side dish aren't worth the trouble. Send steaks back if they're hockey pucks but if you get a medium after ordering medium rare, consider eating it. No one likes to eat with someone who fusses over every little thing. If you must, you can say something after the bill comes.

WHICH FORK?

The rule for cutlery is to work your way from the outside in, matching each piece with each course of food. At the best restaurants you'll have three forks. The outermost one is for appetizers. The second one is for salads. The one closest to your plate is for the main course. Soup spoons are placed on the right outside the knife. If you see a small fork or spoon above your plate, that's for desserts or coffee.

GLASSWARE—HOLDING A WINE GLASS

The long stems on wine glasses aren't just for show; they're for holding. The reasoning goes if you're holding the bulb of the glass the heat from your hand is heating up the wine. And yes, it makes a difference. Hot hands can warm wine fairly quickly and red wine should be served at 74° F (23°C). Any higher and the real taste of the wine will be masked behind a sharp bite that isn't pleasant.

FOOD MASTER CLASS: SUSHI, SOUP, SPAGHETTI

Some foods are trickier to eat than others. Some have their own specific rules that you're just suppose to know about. Sushi, soup, and spaghetti fall into both categories.

Sushi

Eating sushi flies in the face of typical food manners but doing it the wrong way will reveal cultural shortcomings. Essentially there are two things to keep in mind: Use fingers or chopsticks—never a fork—and put the entire piece of sushi in your mouth at once. Biting it in half is unacceptable, even if the piece is huge.

Soup

Soup eating is all about preventing untoward noises. Don't slurp and never lift the bowl to your mouth to down the last bits. Just tilt the bowl away from you and spoon in the rest of it.

Spaghetti

Eating this Italian staple has sent many a fine suit to the dry cleaners so watch out for the splatters. The right way to eat long pasta doesn't necessarily prevent splattering but it's still the right way. Twirl the pasta on a fork, using a large spoon as a guide. And *mama mia!* don't cut it with a knife and fork.

SELECTING WINE

If you're a man plagued by indecision then walking into a well-stocked wine shop will likely paralyze you from the brain down. The same probably happens when it comes to choosing a complement to the main course at a romantic restaurant to impress your date. To avoid feeling verklempt over the vino and to start acting like a man who knows his vineyards, you only have to do one thing: start drinking.

BE A GENTLEMAN: WINE SELECTING TIPS

- ☑ If you're totally flummoxed at the wine store, choose a wine with a cool label. If the juice isn't quite up to par, at least you'll retain an element of gentlemanly charm and style.

- ☑ Don't take a $40 bottle of wine to a house party when you can get a perfectly good $10 bottle. No one's going to notice the difference.

- ☑ At restaurants, tell your server what you like and let them guide you through the wine list.

- ☑ "House" wines at restaurants are typically safe bets.

- ☑ Don't spend too much time ignoring your date and geeking out with the resident sommelier on grape varietals, aging techniques, and the plight of the cork tree in Portugal.

The sooner you know what kinds of wines you like, the more nimble you'll be in front of a dauntingly huge wine list. This may take some time and not a few hangovers. And that's okay, as long as you're taking notes for at least the first hour of drinking. After that, it's more polite to put away the pen and pad and start getting drunk with aplomb.

One key thing to notice while you're sampling is the grape type. Cabernet Sauvignon, Merlot, Pinot Noir, Chardonnay, Sauvignon Blanc, Mourvèdre, and Gewurztraminer are all examples of wine grapes. Many of the world's wine-producing regions will print the name of the grape on the wine label. French wines typically do not, opting instead to name the region of France in which the wine was made (Bordeaux, Loire, Côtes du Rhône, etc.). When tasting wine from that part of the world, you'll need to know which grapes are grown in which regions.

TASTING WINE

There are two different types of wine tasting. Tasting a wine that you've just ordered at a restaurant is far different than attending a wine tasting in which you sample several different grape varietals and explore their tastes and origins. When your server pours you a small "taste" at a restaurant, he or she is not waiting for you to sample the wine to see if you like it or not, they're giving you the opportunity to see if the wine is "good" (i.e. that it hasn't turned to vinegar in the wine cellar). A wine tasting on the other hand can be a fun afternoon out and a great way to get to know different types of wines.

How to Taste Wine at a Restaurant

1   At a restaurant there's always the possibility that the bottle of wine you order is "corked" or "off"—both terms to mean the bottle has gone bad because air has at some point leaked into the bottle past the cork and spoiled the liquid.

2   Servers give you the opportunity to check for this rare chance by pouring you a small sip of wine after presenting the bottle to you table side.

3   Once a small bit of wine is in your glass, smell it. Many wine aficionados will be able to sniff the tell-tale vinegar or rotting fruit without having to taste.

4   If you're not seasoned at smelling wine, give it a taste. The flavor of off wine is unmistakable. It has a vinegary flavor along with a sharp sour bite.

5   If you suspect a bad bottle, simply let your server know you think the wine is corked. He or she will probably get a glass and a sip for themselves to confirm. Then they'll get you a fresh bottle.

6   Don't be embarrassed in these situations. In fact, this gives you the opportunity to show off your refined wine knowledge.

HOW TO TASTE WINE AT A WINE TASTING

1   Notice the color of the wine. Yes, it's easy to tell the difference between red, white, and rosé, but some reds are darker than others and some whites are paler than others. Older red wines take on a lighter tone where newer ones are a deeper purple. Older whites are darker than their younger cousins.

2   Look for the legs. No, not the legs of the hostess pouring the wine. The wine legs. Swirl the wine in the glass and watch the wine run down the inside of the glass. The longer and slower the legs run, the denser the wine will be. That means it will most likely be well aged.

3   Smell the wine. Wine connoisseurs often talk of a wine's "nose." A good whiff should reveal subtle but recognizable smells like flowers, honey, vanilla, or citrus. Like color and density, a wine's nose is another way to get to know it.

4   Taste the wine by sipping a generous portion and swirling it around in your mouth. Notice sweetness or acidity. Usually the more acidic a wine the more tannins it has. Mature, finely-crafted wines will have a good balance between sweetness or "fruit" and tannins.

5   Finally notice the aftertaste. For many wine experts it's preferable that the wine have a long slow aftertaste. The best wines will leave this kind of lasting impression.

HOW TO GIVE A TOAST

For many men the extent of a good toast is "cheers" at the pub.
For a gentleman, lifting a glass and saying a few eloquent words
at the dinner table is a chance to inspire.

How to Give a Toast

1	When the time comes, make sure everyone has a drink to toast with.
2	Get everyone's attention. Clinking your glass with a fork is the traditional announcement that a toast is at hand.
3	Hold your right arm and glass straight out in front of you. Be sure to look the recipient of your words in the eye.
4	When it's time to touch glasses with everyone at the table, look each person in the eye as you toast them with your glass.

MIND YOUR MANNERS: "CHEERS" NOT JEERS

- [X] Don't talk in a whisper so that no one can hear you.
- [X] Try not to talk with a quiver in your voice—if you're nervous, practice at home beforehand.
- [X] Don't go on for too long. Your toast might turn into a sermon and people will start looking around for more booze.
- [X] Never give a toast when drunk.
- [X] Don't go on about a friend's indiscretions in front of large crowds.
- [X] Weeping should be avoided.
- [X] Never talk about your last girlfriend or ex-wife during a toast to your current girlfriend or wife.

If time is short, consider giving a toast in a foreign language. It displays your worldliness while also offering a bit of fun.

- ♦ *Prost* (German)
- ♦ *Kanpai* (Japanese)
- ♦ *Santé* (French)
- ♦ *Sláinte* (Irish Gaelic)
- ♦ *L'Chaim* (Hebrew)
- ♦ *Salud* (Spanish)

WHAT TO DO IF YOU'VE DRUNK TOO MUCH

Having one too many at dinner or during a wine tasting is understandable, especially if the conversation and the wine conjure up the sublime. If you find yourself too tipsy, take some precautions—all the impressions you've worked so hard to cultivate can be dashed with one slip of the tongue, one stumble, or one lost lunch. If you're too drunk to know that you're tipsy, you'd better hope that a good friend can work damage control for you.

MIND YOUR MANNERS: WHEN YOU'VE HAD ONE TOO MANY

- ☒ Talk as little as possible.
- ☒ Call a taxi and leave as soon as possible.
- ☒ Don't give a toast.
- ☒ Don't drive.
- ☒ Leave all your clothes on, including your tie.
- ☒ When the time comes to walk, set goals for yourself—first get to the next table, then to the door, then to the front steps, and so on.
- ☒ Aside from a brief as possible "thanks" do not attempt to thank your host now. Call, e-mail, or write a letter later.

SMOKING CIGARETTES: WHEN IT'S COOL AND WHEN IT ISN'T

Alas, smoking is not as gentlemanly as it used to be. It is rare these days that a puff of smoke equals an air of sophistication. That said, if you do smoke and everyone you're out with lights up, feel free. What you don't want to do is excuse yourself and step out in front of the restaurant alone to have a stogie. It gives the impression of being a desperate addict rather than a gentleman with a sense of manners. Even if half the party smokes and the other half doesn't, resist your urge. No one is going to fault you for not smoking but the one half that doesn't smoke will think less of you for lighting up.

SPLITTING THE BILL

It can be stressful to split a dinner bill, but in large parties it's assumed that everyone is going to pay their way. In large groups, avoid grabbing the bill first and having to play banker by calling out everyone's payment. Better to grab the bill and ask "shall we split it up evenly?" A gentleman should always be happy to split the bill in a large group. Not so when you're out on a date. In those cases, as a gentleman you should always pay even if she wants to cover her portion. However, if she insists on paying next time, allow her. With today's changed gender roles in full effect, there's no shame in sharing the pleasure of taking someone out on a date. Some women may in fact be offended if they're refused the chance to pay.

BEING THE PERFECT HOST

As the host of a party, a gentleman must make sure the evening goes off without a hitch. Putting out drinks and food and getting a bunch of friends together is one thing. Keeping the conversation lively, the music great, and the drinks and dinner plates full all at the same time is another. If you can pull all that off with aplomb, then you've created a masterpiece people will talk about for weeks after.

SUPPLIES

If you throw lots of parties, don't get caught flat-footed so that you're having to scramble around for eight hours in preparation. Keep some essential food, drink, glassware, dishes, and cookware around the house.

HOW MUCH FOOD AND DRINK FOR THE BIG PARTY?

Rule number one for parties with food and drink is you must never run out. That's so much easier said than done but it's a challenge every gentleman should meet. Consider:

- ♦ Is this going to be dinner for your guests? If so, you're going to want more filling food than just nibbles.

- ♦ The more choices you have, the smaller the portions can be.

- ♦ Always round up when you're estimating how much.

- ♦ Add in some hearty, filling foods, such as potatoes and bread.

- ♦ Limit drinks to one or two types, such as beer and wine, martinis, eggnog and wassail, and so on. Don't forget to provide soft drinks for those driving or who don't drink.

PROFESSIONAL CATERING

If you're going to get some help for a big party, hiring caterers is money well spent. They'll take care of the food and drink—everything from estimating how much to making and serving it. They'll also pass around hors d'oeuvres, fill wine glasses, and play bartender. Then at the end of the night they'll clean up the empties and take out the trash. Finding a good caterer is a lot like finding a good handyman. Get recommendations from friends. If you have no luck there, try calling local cooking schools or your favorite restaurant in town. They're bound to know a good caterer and they might do it themselves. Once you've gotten a few good recommendations, call and ask about the style of food they serve, prices, and how long they'll stay at the party. Remember to inquire about any extras like ice, cutlery, or tips. Some things you might be able to supply yourself at a lower cost. Then again, some gentlemen prefer to let the caterers do everything, leaving them to the important task of entertaining and hosting the guests.

SNACKS AND NIBBLES

For big parties or small, ones that serve dinner or just hors d'oeuvres, or even casual get-togethers with no main course, always keep a few snacks and nibbles about the place. These don't have to be fancy but you should try to do better than a bowl of potato chips. Here are a few to consider:

- ♦ Nuts, such as cashews and peanuts.
- ♦ Cheese rounds and various crackers.
- ♦ Olives, black, green, or stuffed.
- ♦ Bite-sized chocolates.
- ♦ Tortilla chips and salsa.

CLEANLINESS IS MANLINESS

A party at your pad will never be what you want it to be if the bathroom hasn't been swabbed in a couple of weeks and the dishes are piled in the sink. Just as you pay attention to your personal appearance you should pay attention to what your place looks like. People are going to take away impressions here too. In other words, getting everything clean is a must.

Usually, doing a total house clean is a big job so either get up and do it in the morning of your event or do it the night before (the place isn't going to go to sod overnight). If you don't have time for the clean, hire a maid. There are maid services everywhere and they're worth the $80 or $100 it's going to take to scrub your house from top to bottom. Who knows, you might even get hooked on having someone else clean for you and hire them back. Usually the price drops the more frequently they come.

SENDING INVITATIONS

A gentleman sending invitations is acceptable but tricky. It's generally smirked upon for a guy to go all-out with formal invites ("Mr. Martin requests the pleasure of your company," etc.) when a woman isn't also involved (read: wedding). Partly, one wonders where a man gets the time to print and address such packets. And partly, one wonders if the sender isn't being a bit effete. That doesn't mean you can't send something fun, irreverent, or perfectly sophisticated for a dinner party, birthday celebration, or dance blow-out. E-mail invitations have become a popular and easy option but your creativity is limited. Better is a postcard-style mail-out that you can design on your computer. People feel so much more special when they open their mailbox and take out a real letter.

> ### MIND YOUR MANNERS: AVOID SENDING...
>
> - [X] Envelopes filled with flower petals or glitter.
> - [X] Anything with glitter involved.
> - [X] Shiny stickers tucked into cards.
> - [X] Cards sprayed with cologne.
> - [X] A picture of you.
> - [X] An invitation that your mother has written.
> - [X] Food, especially the kind that needs refrigerating.

THE GUESTS ARE ARRIVING. WHAT NOW?

The first thing you should do is take their coats and offer them a drink—simple enough. Things get trickier when you start having to remember names. It's always impressive to know a little something about everyone at your party, so you can offer nuggets of information when you introduce people to kick-start their conversations. "Alan Greene, this is Jane Barclay," you might say. "She just got back from the coast. Alan is an avid fisherman." That should be enough to get them going so you can withdraw and work the rest of the room.

On the flip side it's also your job to keep certain guests apart. If you see a friend cornered by someone who won't stop talking, get in there and break up the logjam. And don't just let quiet folks wander around aimlessly. Bring them into the fold and make sure they're having fun. In the meantime, enjoy yourself. There's nothing worse than a host who won't get over the fact that the caterers set the dining room table on fire. Besides, it's not a party until something gets broken.

YOUR SIGNATURE COCKTAIL

A signature cocktail is an impressive addition to a host's repertoire. However, mixing "your drink" when you don't actually drink alcohol lacks credibility. This is the kind of thing you have to love and enjoy to get right, and you can't get a drink right unless you taste it—a lot.

HOW TO MIX A CLASSIC MANHATTAN

You will need

- [✓] American whiskey
- [✓] Sweet vermouth
- [✓] Bitters

Pour whiskey and vermouth over ice in a shaker. The correct proportions vary with taste: the classic is three shots of whiskey to one shot of vermouth, but add more whiskey if you prefer your drink sour. Add a few drops of bitters. Shake, and strain into a cocktail glass. Garnish with a cherry.

How to Mix the Perfect Martini

You will need

- ☑ Gin (vodka can be substituted)
- ☑ Dry vermouth
- ☑ Olives

Pour two shots of gin over ice and stir, so the gin doesn't bruise. Take the vermouth down from the shelf. The next step is to strain the gin into the glass, drop in two olives, and serve the drink, all while thinking about—but not touching—the vermouth.

How to Mix a Man's Margarita

You will need

- ☑ A fine tequila, usually a reposado or aged one is best
- ☑ Fresh limes
- ☑ Cointreau
- ☑ Orange juice

In a large glass or drink shaker pour two shots of tequila, a shot of Cointreau, the juice of three limes, and a splash of orange juice. Cover the glass or shaker and shake well. Place ice in two highball glasses and strain the cocktail over the ice. Garnish with a lime wedge.

How to Open a Bottle of Wine

Opening a bottle of wine is simple enough. You simply have to know how to get the cork out without breaking it or making too much noise. Don't show off an expensive wine, just set the bottle down on the table with the label facing your guests after you've poured, so they can see what they're drinking. These kind of details make a true gentleman.

You will need

- ☑ A bottle of wine
- ☑ "Waiter's friend" folding corkscrew

1. With the knife on your wine opener, cut the top off the plastic sleeve that covers the cork.

2. Using your index finger as a guide, push the tip of the corkscrew into the center of the cork and screw in one or two rotations.

3. Finish screwing in the corkscrew by turning it—no need to press down at this stage, the screw should pull itself into the cork.

4. When the corkscrew is all the way into the cork, tilt the tool up so that the bottle opener on one end fits on top of the bottle lip.

5. Grab the neck of the bottle with your left hand so that you're holding the bottle opener in place on the bottle lip.

6. Pull straight up on the wine tool. Resist pulling over as this might break the cork.

7. Once the cork is most of the way out, grab the whole tool and the cork with one hand and ease it silently out of the bottle.

How to Open a Bottle of Champagne

Champagne is a little more tricky than wine though it doesn't require anything other than your hands to open. And for lots of people, a champagne cork popping out of the bottle is a traditional sound of celebration. Just don't let the cork fly off into the air towards a window, a fragile vase, or your girlfriend's mother's eyeglasses. Champagne should always be served chilled and a gentleman should never shake the bottle before opening—the spray is a waste of perfectly good booze.

You will need

 A bottle of champagne

 Nerves of steel

1   Remove the foil over the top of the champagne cork. There should be a small piece of plastic embedded into the foil to help you do this. Once the foil is off you'll see the cork, covered by a wire "cage" that prevents the cork from shooting out of particularly bubbly champagnes.

2   Place one thumb firmly on top of the cork and the cage while untwisting the cage at the base of the cork. The thumb is a safety measure to prevent the cork from shooting out as you loosen the cage.

3   Once the cage is off, place your right hand over the cork and hold it still while twisting the bottle. The pressure will cause the cork to work its way out.

4   It won't take much but get ready for a surprisingly forceful pop when the cork comes all the way out. Have a glass nearby to catch any overflow so it doesn't go to waste!

WHAT TO DO WHEN YOU GET
A GIFT YOU DON'T LIKE

Parties, especially birthday parties, often mean gifts. It would be great
if we loved every gift we received. Great but impossible. In fact, 60
percent of the time we get gifts that invoke reactions like "what were
they thinking?" and 30 percent of the time we get items that we think
we could learn to love with an alteration here or some paint there. It's
only a meager 10 percent of gifts we get that we can say they are
spot on. So, there's a good chance someone is going to give a gift you
don't like. And when they do, the gentlemanly thing to do is to say
thank you anyway. Send a card. You don't have to lie and say you love
it and plan to put it on your mantelpiece. Just let them know how
thoughtful it was of them to think of you and leave it at that. Bad gifts
are, after all, not reasons to end friendships.

WRITING THANK YOU NOTES

If you have received a gift, try to write a thank you card within a week
from getting it. If your schedule doesn't allow for that, better late than
never is the rule. The note should start off by saying thank you for the
book or knife or whatever it is you received. After that let the person
know how you plan to use it or how it fits into your daily life. If you
don't like the gift you got, focus instead on how thoughtful the person
was to give it to you. It doesn't do anyone any good to say how the gift
isn't quite right. As a gentlemanly touch have
some classy business-sized cards printed with
nothing but your full name on them and include
them in the thank you card. It's an old-fashioned
touch but one others will enjoy.

BEING THE PERFECT GUEST

Oscar Wilde once said "a man who can dominate a London dinner table can dominate the world." In other words, being a good guest is no picnic. Make sure to address the following details so you'll keep your social life going strong.

HOW TO RECEIVE AN INVITATION

What you don't want to do when getting an invitation is call up the host and gush about how flattered and excited you are about the upcoming event. That's not cool. Simply check your calendar and make sure you're not already booked. If you can make it, go ahead and send a polite RSVP e-mail or quick phone call to say that you'll make it.

WHAT TO TAKE: GREAT GIFT IDEAS FOR ALL OCCASIONS AND PEOPLE OF ALL AGES

There is a host of acceptable items to present upon your arrival as a guest. Bringing nothing is not an option. The standard gift for any party is a bottle of wine. The problem is that bringing wine has become so standard that it can sometimes seem a little thoughtless. Try selecting a nice bottle, especially for a dinner party. Flowers are always acceptable too and that ups the ante a little without appearing overbearing. What you bring, however, is often based on what kind of event you're attending. Here's a small list of events and a few gift suggestions to consider.

Occasion	What to bring	What not to bring
Romantic dinner for two, first date	flowers	jeweled necklace or ring
Romantic birthday, dinner for two when in a relationship	a fun and fashionable beaded necklace or bracelet found at a boutique jewelry store	T-shirt, subscription to *Sports Illustrated*
Dinner party	fine olives and bread	rack of lamb, steaks, veggie kabobs, or any main course that's going to be a "surprise" to the host
Birthday party	box of chocolates or truffles	"gag" gifts about how old a person is getting
Rowdy house party	digital play list or music mix burned to CD	flowers
Holiday party	spiced wine, roasted chestnuts, eggnog	box of coal
Spring afternoon get-together	bottle of sparkling lemonade, jar of local honey	Marilyn Manson CD
Graduation of male friend or friend's son	a book on life after college or gentlemanly etiquette or the lost arts of being a man	a book about the disintegrating economic prospects for young graduates
Child's birthday party	a wooden toy or children's book	toys that make noise, violent action video

HOW TO BE THE PERFECT DINNER GUEST

There is no manual to being the perfect guest for the very same reason that there's no script for dinner conversation. Gentlemen who impress fellow diners and give their hosts reason to be proud have an ability to encourage interesting conversation by asking pointed questions, proffering cultural references, and developing the topic for deeper relevance. Good guests resist talking about themselves too much, unless the host prods them into describing to the rest of the crowd their recent Kenyan safari or other amusing or unusual experience. They do not dominate the conversation. They are gracious and funny but they are also good listeners. Manage all this and receiving the next dinner invite will be a matter of when, not if.

SAYING THANK YOU

Hosting a dinner party is a monumental effort, which is why when you get invited to one it's important both to arrive with an appropriate gift, and to present the host or hostess with a sincere thank you after the event. In these cases, a phone call or e-mail saying how much you enjoyed yourself and how great the food was (even if it wasn't) is the preferred vehicle for your gratitude. Thank you cards are best left for those receiving gifts.

CHAPTER
4

THE
FAIRER
SEX

IN THIS CHAPTER YOU'LL LEARN

❖ How to woo with flair ❖ The correct way to behave in female company
❖ When to call ❖ When to kiss ❖ Bedroom manners
❖ The art of buying presents ❖ Etiquette for meeting the parents
❖ How to ask for her hand in marriage

HOW TO WOO WITH FLAIR

The verb "to woo" comes from the Middle English word *wowen*, which may also be where the word "wow" comes from. It means "to seek the affection of with the intent to marry." A more modern definition might be "woo: to impress the ladies." Wooing with originality and confidence is a challenge for even the most accomplished gentleman so if this isn't your strong suit, don't worry. It takes practice. A certain number of embarrassing flops are inevitable. The good thing is that many women find embarrassing flops charming. Try a few of these approaches and if things go wrong, give yourself a thumbs up for just trying—who knows, she may too.

 ♦ Serenade her. Even if your voice breaks or squeaks. This may elicit the tried-but-flopped-but-isn't-he-cute attraction.

 ♦ Send her flowers.

 ♦ Ask her to a performance.

 ♦ Let her know that you cook—women love men who cook.

 ♦ Ask a woman to dance.

 ♦ Tell her she has beautiful eyes.

HOW TO ASK A WOMAN OUT ON A DATE

The rule here is play it cool but not too cool. A gentleman should never take a woman for granted by expecting her to want to spend any more time with him than she already does. His confidence should fuel his own sense of success but it should not boil up into a state of conceit. Playing it cool means treating a woman like your peer, even if she's so gorgeous and smart you can imagine worshipping at her feet. There will be plenty of time for that kind of fun after a successful first date. In general when asking a woman out, a gentleman should be direct.

What to say . . .

☑ Would you like to have dinner with me sometime?

☑ I know a great coffee shop nearby if you'd like to grab a cup this afternoon.

☑ I make the best steak frîtes dinner and I'd love to cook it for you sometime.

☑ Will you go out with me sometime?

☑ Would you like to continue our conversation over dinner/ coffee/drinks?

What not to say . . .

☒ You're probably busy but if you aren't would you like to have dinner?

☒ I know you probably don't go out with guys like me but would you reconsider?

☒ You and me. How about it?

☒ I'm short on cash but would you like to go to dinner anyway?

☒ I've had my eye on you for some time.

HOW TO SAY NO

There may come a time in a gentleman's life when there will be more requests for his company than there are days of the weekend. In such wonderful circumstances it may be necessary to turn down suitors. It's also possible that a man will find himself in the thorny position of saying no for reasons beyond the fact that he simply doesn't have the time. In other words, the attraction may not be mutual. This is no time to abandon good manners. It's also no time to soft-shoe around the topic. Don't make false excuses—they'll either be insultingly transparent, or they'll leave your suitor with false hope leading to further embarrassment down the line. Be honest but not mean. Brevity is an honorable goal as well.

HOW TO HEAR NO

In the dating game, there is always risk with reward. The reward is getting to go out with a woman you're interested in. The risk is she'll say no. Remember, appropriate gentlemanly behavior toward women is not what it used to be. Gender roles have changed, which means the dating game has changed. The modern gentleman should always be chivalrous but respectful of women's established positions in society. If she does give you the turn down, don't get angry. Certainly don't weep. Take it with the grace a gentleman shows in any circumstance, even if you detect a false excuse. After all, this is not a referendum on your character. It's just a date. And if the excuse she has for not going out with you is genuine, use your gentlemanly powers of listening to notice. There's always next time.

HOW TO BEHAVE WHEN YOU'RE WITH A WOMAN

Behaving like a gentleman when asking a woman on a date is only the first step towards a successful outing. Once you're in the company of a woman, a whole new set of manners comes into play. No matter how successful and independent they are, most women still love the kind of chivalry that makes them feel respected and flattered. The modern gentleman is more than willing to comply. Try these where the circumstances are appropriate:

- ♦ Hold doors open for her. If the door pulls open, let her through first. If it pushes, walk through and hold it for her.
- ♦ Offer her your arm when walking down the street: her fingers should rest comfortably in the crook of your elbow.
- ♦ Walk between a lady and the gutter to block potential splashes from passing vehicles.
- ♦ Share your umbrella with her if it's raining, and make sure she's covered even if it means you get wet.
- ♦ Offer to walk her home if she's on foot, or to her car if she's driving home.
- ♦ If she's taking public transport, wait with her at the stop/station until her ride arrives.
- ♦ Offer to walk her to the front door if you're sharing a cab or giving her a ride home.

HOW TO PAY A COMPLIMENT

The rule of thumb for complimenting a lady is say what you mean and mean what you say. However, there are times when a well-timed compliment—even when you don't entirely mean it—is the gentlemanly thing to do. For example, telling your girlfriend that she looks great as you're heading out to dinner, even if she doesn't look her best, will bolster her confidence and put her at ease while making you look like a champ. It's a win-win situation.

BE A GENTLEMAN: SOME WINNING COMPLIMENTS

- ☑ You were the prettiest one there.
- ☑ That perfume smells great.
- ☑ You're looking fit.
- ☑ You look great.
- ☑ That was a great story you told tonight.
- ☑ I always have a great time when we go out.
- ☑ Your hair looks great.
- ☑ You have a beautiful house (if you find yourself over there).

DOOR ETIQUETTE
(NOT ONLY FOR THE WOMAN YOU ARE DATING)

Like good table manners, certain subtle but telling actions will impress both men and women and throw a gentleman's good character into sharp relief. Holding a door open for a woman and letting her through first is one such practice—and a classic one at that. In fact, a gentleman should always take the opportunity to hold the door open for any woman or man (kindness has no gender). In urban situations where everyone is rushing into work, including you, even just holding the door slightly ajar after you've gone in shows right intentions.

ROMANTIC DINNERS FOR TWO

Romantic dining has always been a great way to a woman's heart but not if you behave like you're eating barbecue with the boys. Even in the corner bistro, a gentleman should stay attentive, keep his manners, and make sure his date is comfortable. Often, it's up to you to create an easy atmosphere with a little restaurant know-how.

BE A GENTLEMAN: HOW TO BEHAVE AT A ROMANTIC DINNER

- ☑ Ask lots of questions.
- ☑ Don't talk about yourself too much.
- ☑ Don't talk about sporting events unless she has a particular affinity for inter-league play.
- ☑ Brush up on your wine knowledge.
- ☑ Know what kind of food is being served where you're eating and be able to suggest menu items.
- ☑ Make a plan for after dinner but don't be single-minded about seeing it through.
- ☑ Keep the conversation fresh by bringing up current affairs.
- ☑ Always pay the bill—if she insists, let her pay next time.

WHEN TO CALL SOMEONE YOU LIKE

One of the ongoing debates among men is when to call a woman you like. For a gentleman the determining factors are timing and temperament. Most agree that if you've never called the object of your desire before then you don't have to worry too much about timing—just don't call late at night or when you're drunk: in both situations, your behavior will be perceived as unhinged, or worse— stalker-ish. Not good.

Temperament, on the other hand, is the factor about which one should be most concerned. An overly eager attitude is rarely appropriate. For those who have gone out on a successful first date, an over-eager and premature call can spell disaster. On the other hand, while "playing hard to get" sounds cool, it can be a high risk strategy— the lady concerned may not have the patience for games, or may just think you're not interested. The trick is to strike a balance. Opinions vary but a gentleman's behavior should follow the tone of the date—if the date went well he can call the following evening. This affords the right amount of will-he-call tension but avoids the over-eagerness. If you noticed some tension during the date but are nonetheless overcome with infatuation, then wait until the second day before calling, allowing yourself a quick I-had-a-great-time e-mail with a suggestion of "we should do it again sometime." Her response will be eminently telling.

BACK TO YOUR PLACE

If you are lucky enough to end a date at your place, you might want to consider the impression your surroundings give your new flame. For a gentleman living alone, there's always the tendency to be satisfied with the same furniture and decorations he's had since college. That's okay as long as the aforementioned décor isn't tattered, stained, and smelly, and you bring in a few modern upgrades. It's hard to contemplate, but it might be time to get rid of that old "lucky" lounge chair you sit in during big games. Think of your love life. A woman is more likely to want to go to your place more often if the house is dressed as nicely as you are.

BE A GENTLEMAN: WHAT TO GET RID OF

- ✓ Beer can collections.
- ✓ Concert posters.
- ✓ Couches that have had more than 12 beers spilled on them in a one year period.
- ✓ Frying pans with calcified irremovable substances burned into them.
- ✓ Overly stained coffee mugs.
- ✓ Stained towels or any towels three years old or more.
- ✓ Rugs you bought in Mexico in 1998.
- ✓ House plants that died two years ago.
- ✓ Speakers the size of your front door.

WHEN TO KISS HER, WHEN NOT TO KISS HER

Normally, a gentleman knows when to kiss and when not to kiss according to instinct and body language. If you're having trouble tapping into this gut feeling then that could mean it's not the right time. In that case, always remember your manners and be good-humored: any hint of impatience will push her away rather than draw her in.

On the other hand, if you feel it is the right time and you've noticed a few telling signs, lean in and lock lips. Just be sure to take things slow—at least to start with—so you can be sure whatever happens next is what you both really want.

BE A GENTLEMAN: SIGNS THAT IT'S THE RIGHT TIME TO KISS HER

- ✓ Lots of eye contact in close quarters.
- ✓ Her mouth is slightly open and relaxed as she leans ever so slightly toward you.
- ✓ There are significant pauses in the conversation combined with one or both of the above.
- ✓ You ask and she says yes.
- ✓ You've had a great evening and you're sitting on her couch at the end of the night after she invited you in.

MIND YOUR MANNERS: DON'T ATTEMPT A KISS IF . . .

- [X] She suggests going to a crowded club after dinner instead of to a quiet place.
- [X] You lean in and she stands up.
- [X] You suggest coming in for a nightcap and she says "maybe next time."
- [X] She keeps talking about her ex-boyfriend.
- [X] She refers to you as a good friend and asks if your roommate might want to have dinner with her sometime.

BIRTH CONTROL: A GENTLEMAN'S RESPONSIBILITY

Women are taking positions equal to men in the workplace and at home. Many also take the initiative in dating and pillow talk. When it comes to birth control though, you shouldn't assume she'll have means on hand. Some may, but even the most worldly lady will not want to appear loose. A gentleman should assume it's his responsibility to supply the protection. Even if she's taking her own precautions, a gentleman should insist on adding his until the relationship advances and you can talk with more candor. It's not assuming to have condoms in the medicine cabinet. It's gentlemanly.

HOW TO BEHAVE (OR NOT) IN BED

Libidinous encounters are perhaps the only times a gentleman is expected to behave badly. This is not to say he needs to act like a porn star and certainly not treat his partner like one. But the missionary position and a lack of passion in the sack are considered unrefined. A gentleman may like the best clothes and know his way around the finest foods but that doesn't mean he has to be a prig. Take some chances in bed to satisfy your desires but not at the expense of ignoring her needs.

THE MORNING AFTER

The morning after your first night with a new partner is a sensitive time. If you were drunk the night before and temporarily suspended your better judgment, only to discover what you'd done the morning after, then remain calm. Now's not the time to abandon your manners. Do not jump from the sheets and sprint away. Simply put on your clothes and let her know you had a great time last night. If on the other hand, you had a genuinely good time and she did too then there may be a little gas left in the tank. If time doesn't allow, consider a kiss. Then let her know that you had a great time last night. You both may have the urge to set up another date then and there—or at least gauge interest. Good gentlemanly behavior is often difficult in the early hours without the support of your finest suit, but always try to

put your best foot forward. More than one late-night encounter has turned into a lasting, meaningful relationship, so you don't want to spoil those first delicate moments by abandoning your manners.

DEALING WITH AN UNEXPECTED PREGNANCY

While you and your wife or life partner may be toasting the news that you've succeeded in getting pregnant (she with sparkling apple juice), several conflicting thoughts may go through your head if you're confronted with unplanned procreation with a girlfriend. The first may be pride that everything works as it should. The second may be fear that you're not ready to be a father. In any circumstance the key is to keep a level head: don't rush to judgment, and don't abandon all your hitherto well-practiced gentlemanly etiquette. If anything, this is the time you should muster every ounce of good manners and put them to use.

The first thing to do is ask how your girlfriend is feeling. Is she scared and unsure or overjoyed? It's okay to say that you don't know how you feel. But don't check out all together, and most definitely don't pretend it's her problem. Gentlemanly etiquette requires that you support your partner in this time of need. That doesn't necessarily mean you should announce marriage immediately, declaring "I'll make a great father." Deal with her emotions and yours. Go to the doctor together for an official confirmation. Take a few days to think about all your options and talk them through with your girlfriend. If a gentleman can manage to face his fears and stand by his partner's side throughout tough situations like these, his character will grow beyond all expectations. If this is a situation you don't want to face, see the section on birth control (page 87) and take charge long before your girlfriend announces that her period is late.

PRESENTS: WHEN TO GIVE THEM
AND WHAT TO GIVE

When nights out and sleepovers do develop into relationships, there is a whole new etiquette of which a gentleman should be aware. While public holidays do not require a token of your affection, you'd be surprised how thrilled your girlfriend or wife would be if you got her a gift on random days. It's not required but a gentleman tends to do more than what's required of him. That said, it's not fair for either party to expect such random gifts. Nor is it fair to expect a diamond ring or gold watch on every birthday. There are plenty of things you can give—and plenty of traditional days on which to give them—to make a woman feel special. As a rule, get her anything that will make her feel beautiful.

BE A GENTLEMAN: WHAT TO GIVE AND WHEN

- [✓] **Any occasion:** flowers or chocolates.
- [✓] **First date:** flowers.
- [✓] **Picnics:** a book of poetry.
- [✓] **Romantic outings on the town:** a flower, balloon, or other tidbit.
- [✓] **Anniversaries or birthdays:** jewelry or perfume.
- [✓] **Christmas:** art.
- [✓] **Work success:** massage or afternoon at the spa.

LIVING WITH A WOMAN

It's hard for a man who's used to living alone or with other guys to switch to living with a woman. Usually, it means saying goodbye to the concert posters, the leg lamp, and the collection of Star Wars action figures, or at least banishing them from the bedroom. They may in fact end up in a box in the garage until you can get a "manspace"—a room or shed that's all yours, to do with as you please, and no girls allowed.

But until then there's no reason the house needs to become one big flowered and pastel-colored Easter egg. Work with your new partner as best you can. It's not going to be easy so be prepared to relinquish most of the control, and take pleasure in small décor victories such as a nice dark leather couch in the TV room, space for your tools in the garage, and plenty of room on the bookshelf for your collection of vintage science fiction paperbacks and popular science manuals. If all this sounds too horrible to contemplate, bear in mind that your partner may not be wild about rearranging her belongings either. Some gentlemanly negotiations may be required.

The details of your living arrangements should be worked out between you and your new partner, but bear in mind that the modern gentleman should be just as happy doing the dishes as putting up shelves, as long as the labor is evenly divided. After all, flexibility is an important part of good manners. Be prepared to adapt your life to your new domestic situation, and you'll soon discover that living as a couple has its own rewards.

GETTING ENGAGED—GETTING A RING, ASKING
HER FATHER, GOING DOWN ON ONE KNEE

Asking a lady for her hand in marriage is an exciting step in a gentleman's life and one that requires some sure footing. Know first that this is what you truly want to do (and not just an attempt to appease a strong-willed girlfriend). Know also that engagement leads to marriage—not "eventually" or "some day" or even "in a couple of years." Once the question is popped your wedding plans will begin the very next day, and the date will likely be set within 12 months.

To ask a woman to be your bride takes some planning and strategy. First, you'll need an engagement ring. The rule on how much to spend is that the ring should cost roughly the equivalent to two months' salary. The ring should be a diamond. How the rock is set will be up to your individual tastes, though a single solitary diamond is traditional. Know also you'll need to choose between silver, gold, white gold, and platinum for the ring band. Platinum is the most expensive.

Once you have the ring you'll then need to ask her father for his blessing. This is an old-fashioned thing to do but it still offers a valuable rite of passage as well as the opportunity to get in good standing with your future in-laws. There is, however, a warning: do make sure your bride is happy for you to ask her father. Your loyalty is to her first and if for any reason she doesn't want to involve him in her decision, even as a formality, then you have to respect her wishes. She'll still think the world of you for even wanting to speak to her parents.

If she agrees that you should ask her father, then you're in business. But be warned: this is and should be an intimidating task. When my father went to ask his future father-in-law (my grandfather) for his blessing to marry my mother, my grandfather laid a shotgun on the table and said, "I understand you have something you want to talk to me about." It was a joke, of course, but my grandfather made my dad sweat it out first.

BE A GENTLEMAN: HOW TO ASK HER FATHER FOR HER HAND

1   Start with a phone call. If you've never met the man, politely introduce yourself.

2   Tell him you're coming to town for a visit and ask if you can drop in to speak to him about an important matter. The mysterious nature of your visit is a good thing. He probably has in mind what this is all about.

3   Put on your best clothes—a nice suit and dress shirt with no tie is appropriate.

4   When he answers the door don't blurt out "I want to marry your daughter!" Wait until the pleasantries have been exchanged and then ask if you and he can talk alone.

5   Then come out and say, "Mary and I want to get married and I've come to ask for your blessing."

6   Some questions may ensue such as "Is she pregnant?" "Do you love her?" or "Do you have a job?" Prepare in advance for these.

7   Once he gives his blessing, say thank you. Hug your future mother-in-law and take your leave.

POPPING THE QUESTION

Once the idea has been put to her parents, a gentleman should not wait long before officially asking for his lady's hand in marriage. Though gender roles have changed and the professional and romantic landscape looks far different for men today than it did fifty years ago, a gentleman should still get down on one knee and propose. It's both chivalrous and respectful. You and she will remember it always. Also, choose a memorable spot to ask the question. A favorite restaurant is good—as long as you don't mind everyone staring at you. It's better to get creative. In a hot-air balloon, atop the Empire State Building, or at the beach are all good—anywhere that underscores how special the moment is.

MEETING YOUR GIRLFRIEND'S/WIFE'S PARENTS

Many a breakup has followed a visit to the parents' home. That's because one of the unwritten and unfair laws of dating is that when you meet your girlfriend's parents for the first time your girlfriend will also inspect you from top to toe as if you'd never met. Whether she knows it or not, your girlfriend will judge you through her parents' eyes when you set foot in the home of her childhood. How to behave in these situations is really no different than any other event loaded with pressure that a gentleman may encounter. Be on your best behavior so you can leave a solid first impression. Hold yourself with pride to emit confidence and be on your conversational toes so you can both talk and listen politely to your hosts. What your partner is looking for is whether or not you are genuinely yourself around these people who have had such a profound effect on her life. One surefire way to ease the tension is to bring her mother flowers. But only do this if you've actually given your girlfriend flowers a few times before.

REMEMBERING DATES

To remain that attentive, considerate gentleman who swept her off her feet in the first place, start with remembering important dates, such as her birthday and your anniversary. These are the kinds of details that tend to slip between the cracks if left only to memory. And yes, they are important. Too busy? That excuse never works.

For busy gentlemen the key to remembering dates is to get a computer, hand-held organizer, or some other gadget equipped with a calendar and reminder facilities, or failing that a good old-fashioned diary. The trick is to get the important dates on your calendar as soon as you know what they are: if she's told you when her birthday is, she's going to expect you to remember. Jotting it down or putting it on your calendar takes ten seconds and can save you hours of explaining. It can also be helpful to set your device to warn you at least a couple days before the date to remember. That way you'll have time to prepare: make a reservation at a nice restaurant, order some flowers to be delivered to her, or buy a present (see page 90 for some ideas). After all, sooner or later a card and simple best wishes aren't going to be enough.

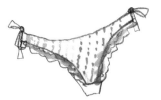

CHAPTER
5

MEN
AT
WORK

IN THIS CHAPTER YOU'LL LEARN

✦ How to behave in a job interview ✦ Dress and etiquette for business
meetings, elevators, and parties ✦ The pitfalls and rewards of office dating
✦ Business phone and e-mail etiquette ✦ How to give the perfect presentation
✦ Manners for the business lunch

THE JOB INTERVIEW

There are entire books written about job hunting, with long prominent chapters dedicated to good performance in a job interview. Really, all a gentleman needs to impress prospective employers is to stick to his etiquette. Dress your best to leave a good first impression, prepare beforehand, and give substantive answers, listen attentively so you can ask in-depth questions, and speak with self-confidence to drive home that strong first impression.

BE A GENTLEMAN: INTERVIEW ETIQUETTE

- ☑ Dress conservatively, even if you're applying for a creative position at a dot-com startup.

- ☑ Look your interviewer in the eye when you shake his or her hand.

- ☑ Smile a lot.

- ☑ Know everything you can about the company and the position for which you are interviewing. Knowledge breeds confidence. You can start with their Web site.

- ☑ Ask your interviewer questions. This shows you're engaged in the process and prepared, especially if they are challenging questions (although challenging should never become argumentative).

- ☑ Write a professional follow-up e-mail later in the day or first thing in the morning. Make sure your spelling and grammar are perfect.

OFFICE ETIQUETTE

Gentlemanly behavior is just as important at work as with the fairer sex, except that here it affects your paycheck rather than your love life.

WHAT TO WEAR TO THE OFFICE

Office etiquette always starts with how you dress. Suits and ties are no longer the work day uniform they used to be but it's not all shorts and T-shirts either—especially with more women in the workplace, all of them dressed to the nines. A gentleman should always try to look his

---

MIND YOUR MANNERS: WHAT NOT TO WEAR AT THE OFFICE

- [X] Shorts.
- [X] Jeans with holes in them, even if the jeans and their carefully designed holes cost you $150.
- [X] T-shirts with obscene lyrics or illustrations on them.
- [X] Turtleneck sweaters.
- [X] Baggy clothes.
- [X] Bandanas on your head.
- [X] Flip-flops.
- [X] Leather (except in belts or shoes).
- [X] Cologne.
- [X] Sunglasses.

best at work. Co-workers will take you more seriously. Customers and clients will too. Luckily there are a whole new set of fashion options for the working gentleman that go beyond the pin-striped suit. "Business casual" is the name the fashion world has created for this new category of work attire. This usually consists of a nice pair of pants (not usually jeans), a collared button-down shirt, and some comfortable shoes. Of course, variations on this are numerous. The general rule is that your dress should be in line with what others of similar standing wear at your office. Financial planners and young attorneys will, after all, have a different standard of dress than graphic designers and record producers.

HOW TO BEHAVE IN A BUSINESS MEETING

Giving others a chance to be heard is standard etiquette for a gentleman wherever he is. In workplace meetings, this is especially true. One of the unwritten rules at business meetings is everyone must say something, and the younger or less experienced employees must say something before the older, more experienced employees. That's because younger employees can get intimidated and clam up if older employees speak up first. Most important for a young gentleman just starting out in a new job is to get engaged in the office culture. One great way to do that is to speak up at meetings even if what you're saying isn't particularly edifying. Asking sensible questions is a good way to do this. Of course, a gentleman should always be prepared and on time. Make sure you know what's expected of you and try to offer fresh perspectives. It's also bad etiquette to interfere or cross over into other employees' areas of expertise or responsibility. Do that and you'll invite the ire of co-workers who think you're trying to climb the corporate ladder right past them.

ELEVATOR ETIQUETTE

In any small space full of strangers, appropriate behavior is essential or the whole situation will devolve into miserable claustrophobic chaos. Elevator etiquette is simple: wait for those already on to get off before you get on; allow ladies and the elderly or less able to get on first; and don't cram yourself on if it's already overcrowded. Be aware that many people consider talking loudly on an elevator to be rude, especially cell phone conversations—even if you can get reception.

BE A GENTLEMAN: ELEVATOR ETIQUETTE

- ☑ Don't push through the crowd to get to your floor. Simply say "excuse me," or hold the door and make your way politely to the front.
- ☑ Allow ladies to get off first.
- ☑ If you're standing near the doors and someone needs to get off, get out of the way. It's appropriate to step out of the elevator to do this.
- ☑ If you're waiting for an elevator and you see someone stepping out of the elevator to let people out, allow that person to get back on before walking on yourself.
- ☑ Don't make remarks about people after they get off the elevator. A friend or colleague of theirs could still be riding and listening in.
- ☑ If you're the first on, stand as close as possible to one of the walls.
- ☑ Hold the door for latecomers within reason, but not so much that everyone else on the elevator gets impatient.
- ☑ Be aware of others when you have big bags on an elevator. When traveling with bulky luggage, try to take an empty elevator if possible.

THE HOLIDAY PARTY—WHAT TO WEAR, WHO TO TALK TO, WHAT TO SAY

Gentlemanly behavior at the office should always lean toward hard work and good preparation. But not totally. Knowing how to have fun and make light of certain situations is just as important, and a valuable characteristic in all walks of life. The key is knowing when and when not to bring out the humor. The annual holiday party is an appropriate place to let your personality show, though it's still the office party, which means there is some office-party etiquette to prepare for. A gentleman would never want to end up with his boss's best lamp shade on his head by the end of the night . . .

WHAT TO WEAR

Office parties, especially holiday ones, are an opportunity to bring out your more fashionable wardrobe. Again, let your co-workers see some of your personality, though keep it relatively toned down. Wear a suit or a suit jacket and one of your better shirts to match the festive occasion.

WHO TO TALK TO

Talk to everyone. Make a special effort to talk to your boss and say hello to his or her wife or husband. If you hang out with a particular group at the office, you can see them here too but make an additional effort to get to know those you don't normally talk to.

WHAT TO SAY

When you're talking to new acquaintances use the same small talk etiquette you might use anywhere (see page 19). In these situations you can always ask if someone has plans to travel for the holidays. If you notice a colleague without his or her significant other, it's advisable to avoid asking about them unless you're certain the two are still together. The holidays can present a low point for lots of people and you don't want to rub salt into any open wounds with a thoughtless question.

MIND YOUR MANNERS: HOLIDAY PARTY ETIQUETTE

- [X] Don't arrive hungry—you want to work the crowd not the spread.
- [X] Don't eat without making an occasional trip to the bathroom to check for food in your teeth.
- [X] Don't forget to limit your alcohol intake.
- [X] Don't talk about work.
- [X] Don't bitch about work or co-workers.
- [X] Don't automatically say Merry Christmas—not everyone celebrates the Christian holiday. Say Happy Holidays instead.

The events of the holiday party tend to become legends of office gossip, so it's wise to moderate your behavior and alcohol intake accordingly. Often, members of senior management will be present for the start of the party, but will discreetly withdraw an hour or two into proceedings to allow the rest of the room to relax a bit more. Nonetheless, if you make a fool or yourself, you can guarantee the story will get back to your boss somehow. You have been warned.

DATING AT THE OFFICE—TO DO IT
OR NOT TO DO IT?

Flirty behavior and professional mannerisms don't match. In other words, don't date at the office. Erotic engagements in the course of business negotiations tend to be anything but simple or romantic, no matter how exciting the initial surreptitious encounters may be, and a gentleman put in this complicated position will be hard pressed to keep his wits about him. For example, what if the relationship goes sour? Pessimism isn't a typical gentlemanly characteristic, and certainly not an attractive one, but the breakup question is impossible to ignore when it involves a co-worker. It's certainly the question your boss is going to ask if he notices the two of you holding hands at the photocopier. Likely, a breakup is going to impact on your productivity, and for the two involved it's going to make personal and professional lives miserable.

Those who decline to listen to sage advice or their own better judgment and decide to ignite the spark they've struck in the office break room, should be sure to keep it secret. This can, after all, be part of the attraction. Further secret office affair etiquette is as follows: no public displays of affection; no lengthy bathroom breaks together; if the elevator is getting stuck on a regular basis between floors three and four with the two of you emerging disheveled, people will talk; and finally, if word gets out, be prepared to take your job termination with gentlemanly aplomb—no gnashing of teeth, no threats, and no slamming doors. No one can say you didn't have it coming.

E-MAIL ETIQUETTE

The need to know how to behave online is a growing concern, especially when sending e-mails to co-workers and clients. Though composing an e-mail may seem to have nothing whatsoever in common with the composition of a letter by snail mail (you can see these artifacts at a local history museum), the truth is that the two have more in common than most people realize. Just as if you were meeting a person for the first time, you should display the same kind of introductory manners in a first-time e-mail. Begin with a formal heading, then introduce yourself. When you're done sign off with a traditional ending ("Sincerely," "All best," "Regards") and your name. In the body of the e-mail, be sure and get to the point quickly. However, never forgo a sentence or two of pleasantries before diving into business. Gentlemanly manners are a prerequisite even on the Internet.

BUSINESS PHONE ETIQUETTE

Business contacts, whether long-term or brand new, will form an impression of you whether they meet you face to face or not. Your picture on the company Web site or a bio on a brochure will give enough information for others to make a first judgment. A phone call will also cement a first impression. This is why a gentleman should always be well mannered, regardless of whether he's talking into a headset or to a real person. If you're calling someone for the first time, say your full name, who you work for, and your position. Include the reason for your call. If you have an ongoing relationship, it's still proper to say who you are and who you work for when they first pick up the phone. Other than that, stay on your topic, listen when you need to, and speak clearly. Here are a few more tips:

- Prepare by finding out as much as you can about the person and the company you are calling.

- When dealing with long-term clients, begin with some courteous small talk, such as "How was your weekend?" before launching into the business at hand.

- Be succinct and get to the point quickly.

- Make your intentions clear early on—don't assume the person you're talking to knows why you've called.

- If the phone call grows tense or heated, stay calm and be patient.

- Establish a follow-up call or the next steps toward your mutual goal.

MIND YOUR MANNERS: THE BUSINESS PHONE CALL

☒	Don't call someone for the first time and say "Hi, this is John."
☒	Avoid talking about your wild party weekend.
☒	Don't use words like "Yep" or "Okey-Dokey."
☒	Never fail to listen to what the other person says.
☒	Don't avoid answering questions.
☒	Never hang up without saying good-bye.

WORK SPEAK AND SPEAKING AT WORK

Every industry has its own jargon which is both necessary and effective. The only time you don't want to use it is when you're trying to impress clients who aren't in your field. Then you'll just confuse them. At work though, it's impossible to communicate effectively with co-workers and clients if you don't pick up on the work speak. At no time is this more important than when it's your turn to give a presentation to the rest of the office.

GIVING THE PERFECT PRESENTATION

If you're asked to give a presentation at work you're doing something right. It is likely your boss is confident that you can communicate what needs to be said in the most effective way. Now it's up to you not to let him or her down.

Giving a presentation is a lot like speaking publicly. It can be nerve-wracking and highly pressured. You need to be able to speak clearly and in a lively manner, with good humor. (For pointers on these aspects of speaking in front of crowd see page 22.) A business presentation, however, is a little different in that you're often speaking to colleagues and clients who have a very good understanding of the reasons behind your presentation, and in this way it's much more challenging. You need to give deeper insights, have more original visuals, and leave the attendees with a clear idea of how you and the company can move forward.

Like many things a gentleman does, business presentations begin with preparation. In general, plan it down to the minute. Make sure you have an opening, a middle, and a closing. The opening should grab everyone's attention. The middle should have a series of points each followed by information that backs them up. The closing should wrap everything up with an easily digestible review of your major points. Keep your presentation on the topic. Use some anecdotes to keep from being dull, but not as many as you would when trying to entertain a large crowd (this is business and people have schedules).

You should also check that any equipment you need (microphone, computer projector, flip charts, podium) is in place and operable before you're due to get into the conference room. Then relax, be confident, and have fun with it. Those in the room are more likely to buy what you have to say if you're prepared and enjoying what you do.

THE BUSINESS LUNCH

A gentleman at any eating engagement, whether a business lunch or a date, should follow the standard rules of etiquette (see page 50). For a gentleman dining with his boss or potential clients, there are some additional things to know. A business lunch can be both an excellent opportunity to inspire creative ideas outside the office and a great way to get to know your colleagues.

- Always arrive five minutes before the appointed time. If you rush in only just on time, you come across as being disheveled and disorganized, and people will think that's how you conduct business.

- Turn off your cell phone or pager before lunch. If you forget and do get a call, turn off the ringer without answering it.

- Stand up and shake everyone's hands if you are sitting down before they arrive.

- Order your food before jumping into the business at hand, unless your boss asked you a pointed question straight away.

- Avoid messy, high maintenance foods, such as lobster and barbecue sandwiches. You want to focus on the conversation not your plate.

- Whatever you order, don't wolf your food down. If you have big mouthfuls of food, you won't be able to talk. Give the conversation precedence over your appetite.

- Always be kind and courteous to the servers. No one likes to deal with someone who is rude—even if it's not directed at them personally.

- Don't be the only one to order dessert, especially if you're not the one paying.

- Pay the bill if you're the one who called the meeting or if you're visiting clients in another city.

- Don't ask for a doggy bag. If you're still hungry after the meeting, get something after you've said good-bye to the rest of the people in the lunch party.

CHAPTER
6

THE
GENTLEMAN
AT
LARGE

IN THIS CHAPTER YOU'LL LEARN

❖ How to organize a bachelor party ❖ What to do as best man
❖ Good sportsmanship ❖ Drinking etiquette ❖ How to travel like a
gentleman ❖ Gentlemanly use of technology ❖ Good driving manners
❖ The right way to talk to the police ❖ Gym etiquette

SOCIAL OCCASIONS

Business lunches and romantic dinners are one thing, but it's easy to lose your inhibitions when you're out with your buddies. As a true gentleman, you'll keep your wits and manners about you even in the most informal settings. The rules of thumb you've learned in previous chapters—calmness, self-respect, and respect for others—should keep you on the straight and narrow, but here are a few more tips.

BE A GENTLEMAN: HOW TO HOST A SUCCESSFUL BACHELOR PARTY

- ☑ Plan the evening far in advance. First, make sure you know who the groom wants at the party and then make sure those people will be there.

- ☑ If you're going out to dinner, reserve a private room. A big group of guys in the main dining room of a nice restaurant will only be annoying for everyone else. Plus, it's a great place for a nice (or not so nice) lady to jump out of a giant cake and surprise the groom.

- ☑ Find a giant cake and a nice (or not so nice) lady to jump out of it.

- ☑ Collect everyone's money ahead of time and open tabs at the bars you go to.

- ☑ Tip your bartender and any other entertainers well.

- ☑ Have fun.

THE BACHELOR PARTY

Gentlemen aren't worried about first impressions at a bachelor party but that doesn't mean there isn't an etiquette to these bacchanalia. Rather than knowing which fork to use or why you should keep your elbows off the table, the rights and wrongs veer more toward making sure you don't get thrown in jail or end up with your picture in the paper.

MIND YOUR MANNERS: BACHELOR PARTY NO-NOS

- ☒   Don't have the bachelor party the night before the wedding.

- ☒   Avoid anything that is going to offend the bride . . . too much. This is definitely not the time for the groom to get into a situation that's going to compromise his relationship.

- ☒   Invite the right people. If you're going to invite one person from the groom's office, you should invite everyone. But it's usually not a good idea to invite people the groom doesn't know that well, especially if they're related to the bride. He wants to feel comfortable and relaxed, and probably won't be interested in small talk.

- ☒   Don't let everyone get too drunk too soon. Otherwise, neither the groom nor anyone else will remember what happened after 9 pm, and that can lead to untold debauchery. The evening should be remembered at least until 10 pm.

BEST MAN ETIQUETTE

Being a best man is a great honor, not only because you have a friend who thinks so highly of you that he wants you to be part of a very special time in his life, but also because the job has some important responsibilities. True, it is the best man's responsibility to plan and organize the bachelor soirée, but there are also a few vital things the best man must see through which are going to affect both the bride and the groom.

- Get the groom to the wedding on time and sober.
- Hold the rings.
- Manage the ushers, readers, singers, and flower girls.
- Walk down the aisle with his counterpart on the bride's side of the aisle.
- Give a toast at the wedding party (see pages 60–1 for pointers on good toasts).
- Work the wedding party to make sure everyone is having a good time.
- Make sure the car arrives on time to take the bride and groom away.
- Make sure the facility where the wedding party took place is cleaned and in order.
- Return the groom's rental tux, if necessary.

GOOD SPORTSMANSHIP

Sports often imitate life, so being a gentleman on the gridiron, the court, or the baseball diamond is good practice for playing the right way at the office or in a relationship. Practice, hard work, and respect for the people you're competing against are all good manners when you're in friendly competition with others. It also makes winning that much sweeter.

BE A GENTLEMAN: SPORTMAN'S ETIQUETTE

- ☑ Make sure everybody knows what the rules are before you start the game.
- ☑ Pick on someone your own size.
- ☑ Don't stand and celebrate when someone on the opposing team gets hurt. Lend a helping hand.
- ☑ When the opposing team or player makes a good play, let them know. A simple "nice play" will do.
- ☑ Competition can really boost adrenaline and that can lead to angry confrontations. Try to keep your emotions in check. It's only a game.
- ☑ Always congratulate the opposing team or player whether you win or lose.

HOW TO WATCH SPORTS
WELL WITH OTHERS

Watching sports with your buddies is in many ways similar to playing it. You're rooting for one team to win but others in the room or in the stadium will be rooting for the other team. Gentlemanly behavior, therefore, demands that you don't let things get too tense and aggressive so that friendships are strained and a good time turns bad. Following are a few sports-watching etiquette tips:

MIND YOUR MANNERS: BE A GOOD SPORT

- [X] Don't gloat or be obnoxious when your team makes a good play.
- [X] Acknowledge good plays made by the other team.
- [X] Try not to belittle the opposing team or its players. A lot of emotion is invested into rooting for a home team so criticism can be taken personally.
- [X] Be aware of your companions' moods, and back off if they're starting to get tense.
- [X] Whoever wins, make a point of saying how good the play was on both sides.

HOW TO KNOW WHEN
ENOUGH BEER IS ENOUGH

All men have different tolerances for beer, some with seemingly hollow legs into which they can pour six pack after six pack without feeling a thing, and others with the constitution of a feather, which leaves them light-headed after a glass or two. A gentleman will know his limit, and will be able to gauge the situation appropriately to decide whether or how much he should go past that limit.

YOU KNOW YOU'VE HAD ENOUGH BEER WHEN:

1   You call old girlfriends, old friends, or people you don't know from your cell phone after midnight.

2   The last half of any sentence you say blurs together.

3   You try to get off the bar stool but end up on the floor.

4   Various articles of clothing have come off in public and you're considering taking off more.

5   You strike up heated conversations about heartbreak and girl troubles with cab drivers.

6   You visit the toilet more than three times in 30 minutes.

7   The bartender says they've run out of the beer you were drinking.

8   Your friends have left you behind.

9   More than one person tells you to keep your voice down.

10 The woman you tried to avoid at the beginning of the evening has taken on an attractive aura.

TRAVEL

Whether you're on vacation or a business trip, traveling can be a pleasure or a chore. And rude behavior that offends local people, travel officials, and your fellow passengers is a surefire way to ruin your journey. Make sure not to leave your gentlemanly manners at home, and you'll enjoy your trip that much more.

WHAT TO WEAR ON AN AIRPLANE

Although dressing up for an airplane ride went out well before the in-flight meal, looking sharp while you travel is a particular luxury. Since so many people insist on wearing white tennis shoes and sweats between New York and London, why not stand out in the crowd and look important by putting on a suit jacket? That's not to say one should wear blister-rubbing leather dress shoes and a tie, but it is possible to be comfortable while looking sharp at the same time. Peruse the business casual section of most men's stores and you'll get an idea of the look. Shoes with good support but a trendy finish are everywhere. Even a T-shirt under a suit jacket looks as though you've thought about your appearance. Smart dress and a nice smile when you're checking in may even bag you an upgrade if the flight is quiet. In any case, the interesting thing about flying is that you never know who you're going to meet, so this is no time to let your guard down or lose your gentlemanly polish.

HOW MUCH LUGGAGE TO BRING

A truck-load of luggage is best left to the women in your travel party. For a gentleman, packing more than one suitcase for himself can signal high maintenance, vanity, and indecision. Besides, who wants to haul suitcases all over the airport and then wait around at the baggage carousel for hours to collect their goods? It's best to bring one bag for your clothes, and one for books and papers that you can carry on the plane.

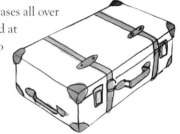

HOW TO ACT IN A FOREIGN COUNTRY

The maxim "when in Rome, do as the Romans do" is as true today as it was in the time of Julius Caesar. Never assume that etiquette and appearances in another country are the same as they are in yours. It's likely that they'll be different. This means a gentleman should try to be as low-key and observant as possible. Try to blend in with the crowd and don't abandon basic good manners. Read up on the country you're visiting and respect all cultural guidelines, whether that means staying away from alcohol (Saudi Arabia) or not wearing shorts in public temples (Thailand). Something as easy as learning how to say "thank you" in the local language can make a surprising amount of difference—if people know you have made an effort, no matter how small, they'll look on you more kindly and welcome you more warmly.

WHAT TO DO ON CROWDED SUBWAY CARS

Navigating rush hour on subways and commuter trains is an art that requires practice. For the uninitiated, being surrounded by bodies on the platform and train can be a bit unnerving. In general, be flexible. Don't stand in the way of the doors. If you're near a door when the train stops and someone behind you wants to get off, step off the train and get back on after those leaving have exited. Work your way into the center of the car, especially if you're traveling more than one or two stops. You're more likely to find a seat that way too, although if there are pregnant women or the elderly or less able around, offer a seat to them before taking one yourself. Lastly, don't chat to other people on the train—most of them won't want to bother with small talk. It is best to read a book or paper, or simply stare into space.

STRATEGIES FOR A SMOOTH RIDE ON A CROWDED SUBWAY CAR

1   Don't keep your wallet stuck in your back pocket. You never know if someone's going to take advantage of the body-to-body contact to remove your belongings.

2   Don't spit on the platform—in some cities you'll get a ticket.

3   Don't let your hands wander onto the lovely lady crammed up against you—you'll get an earful, punched, arrested, or all three.

4   Don't stare.

5   Don't open your newspaper up all the way so that you're invading someone else's space.

OUT AND ABOUT

Sad to say, life isn't one long dinner party. But that doesn't mean good etiquette should be dropped once the night is over and the morning comes. Nor should men forget how to act when the tie comes off after work. But you should know the drill by now . . .

TECHNOLOGY—THE ETIQUETTE OF SWITCHING OFF

Technology has inundated most of what we do, from cell phones to hand-helds, computers to portable music and video players. It's convenient, fun, and cool to be connected. The danger is staying connected so that the technology uses you instead of you using it.

Just like it's bad manners to talk on the phone while trying to order dinner at a restaurant, it's equally offensive to keep your earbuds in through all human contact, or to be talking to somebody with one eye and half your mind on the screen. It's just rude.

Besides, if your technology is always on, your senses are off, and life may pass you by before you've noticed. The same can be said for working late, or plugging into the PlayStation every free moment and letting a social life pass you by. Everything in moderation is the key here. Use your technology wisely and keep a good balance with the real world. Read a novel instead of watching endless reruns. Try a visit to the theater every now and again, instead of the cinema every week. Or try seeing a film dubbed from another language (and no, chop-socky kung fu movies don't count). Even if you hate it, it'll give you something to talk about at your next dinner date.

HOW TO DRIVE IN TRAFFIC
TO AVOID ROAD RAGE

We've all wanted to ram a car that cuts us off, or pull someone over to tell them in explicit detail how bad their driving is. Often we forget all gentlemanly manners on the road, and hand gestures are exchanged while we curse to ourselves before going our separate ways. In extreme cases, a situation can become more heated and result in damage to your car or even fisticuffs. It's not an ideal situation, but driving can do that to a person. To avoid road rage and keep your calm demeanor in the face of idiots behind the wheel, try the following:

♦ Drive by the rules. If you're all over the place or driving too aggressively, others are going to be offended and may try and get in your way.

♦ Don't tailgate, drive excessively slowly, or fail to use your turn signal. These things can make other drivers furious, which can lead to a confrontation.

♦ If you feel yourself getting hot under the collar, try playing some relaxing music.

♦ Let aggressive drivers go on down the road rather than trying to get in their way. Be comforted by the thought that everyone else on the road also thinks they're an idiot.

♦ Forget the notion that everyone else on the road is out to get you. They don't even know you.

HOW TO SPEAK TO
THE AUTHORITIES

Getting pulled over by the police or interviewed by a customs official is no time to abandon your eloquence or honed conversation skills. This could be when they come in handy the most. Know, however, that talking to the authorities is not the same as talking to acquaintances at a cocktail party. They are far less likely, for example, to warm up to you for cracking wise. If you don't want to get the book thrown at you, give plenty of respect and answer honestly and as directly as possible, unless honesty is going to incriminate you. In that case, get a lawyer and don't say a thing. In general, guilty or innocent, the less talking the better.

MIND YOUR MANNERS: AVOID WISECRACKS
LIKE THESE . . .

- [X] Shouldn't you be trying to catch terrorists?
- [X] I'm not a bad person; I was only going ten miles over the speed limit.
- [X] It wasn't my idea.
- [X] Your job must get awfully boring.
- [X] My wife is having a baby at the hospital RIGHT NOW!
- [X] Look, I used to drive NASCAR rallies and I can handle the speed.
- [X] He did it.

GYM ETIQUETTE

Acting like a gentleman will require quite a bit of effort and even a little muscle—especially at the gym. Just make sure that you wipe up when you get off the bench press. No one wants to slip on your sweat. Following are a few more tips you can pack in your gym bag.

♦ Unless it's blatantly obvious she's interested in talking to you, try not to spark up conversation with the good-looking girl doing squat thrusts near the floor-to-ceiling mirror. Women rarely go to the gym to flirt. Those that do will not be doing squat thrusts.

♦ Anyone wearing headphones does not want to have idle chat. Further evidence of this is when they pull only one earbud out. A gentleman knows how to take a hint.

♦ A gentleman should not sing at the gym while listening to music through headphones. In fact, a gentleman should consider not singing at the gym under any circumstances.

♦ Be mindful of those waiting to use the machine you're on.

♦ Hovering, glaring, or otherwise pressuring folks at the gym to hurry up is not gentlemanly behavior. If it really bothers you that they're taking so much time, give them a copy of this book.

♦ Grunting may be okay, to a degree, while playing tennis, but it is unpleasant in the close confines of the gym. Have some reserve, man!

♦ Wipe down and put away equipment when you're done so others can use it. This does not include the towel you've been using to wipe up all your gentlemanly sweat.

CONCLUSION:
THE NEW ETIQUETTE

For a gentleman working, dating, and living in
the new competitive landscape of changing gender
roles, knowing how to behave has never been
more important. One doesn't have to be wealthy,
well-born, or even good-looking to be a gentleman, and being savvy in gentlemanly etiquette
doesn't mean giving up any of your other interests
either (unless being rude and annoying others is your hobby). In fact,
being a gentleman is as much about being proud of who you are as it is
about knowing how to act at the office party. We should, however,
know a few skills to help us show our best faces to the world. That's
why this book, with its insights into which fork to use and its tips on
gift-giving and fashion, can be so helpful. The goal is to re-create the
spirit of the chivalrous deeds of times past, but to combine that
chivalry with a modern sense of respect for the women and men in
our lives.

For lots of guys, acting like a gentleman may seem like a lot of work,
and at first it will be. Over time, though, it will seem as if your true
instincts have been awakened. Then, holding a door open for a lady,
heating up the iron, and speaking in front of large crowds will be as
effortless as trying on a new suit.

INDEX